Praise for Homer's Odyssey

"Touching...one not to miss."

—USA Today

"This memoir about adopting a special-needs kitten teaches that sometimes in life, you have to take a blind leap."

—People

"Cooper is a genial writer with a gift for conveying the inner essence of an animal."

—The Christian Science Monitor

"Delightful...This lovely human-feline memoir, following in the footsteps of Vicki Myron's bestselling *Dewey*, is sure to warm the hearts of all pet lovers."

—Library Journal

"Well written with...tenderness and realism...Your life will be richer for having taken this journey with [Gwen and Homer]."

—I Love Cats **magazine**

Praise for My Life in a Cat House

"This book perfectly encapsulates the unique and amazing experience of being owned by cats and the joy they bring into our lives. That alone is reason enough to read it."
—James Bowen, international bestselling author of *A Street Cat Named Bob*

"Cooper, who charmed readers with the best-selling memoir of her intrepid blind cat, *Homer's Odyssey*, returns with escapades of other past and present felines. Cooper's witty, breezy writing, her unabashed love of felines, and her admission that her spoiled cats have trained her will delight and resonate with cat people."
—*Library Journal*

"Fans of *Homer's Odyssey* will rejoice upon hearing that Homer's owner, Cooper, has returned with more true cat stories...both hilarious and deeply moving. Readers...will delight in these anecdotes of cats who seemingly have something to say about everything. Fans of Vicky Myron and Brett Witter's *Dewey* and James Bowen's *A Street Cat Named Bob* will be highly satisfied."
—*Booklist*

"If you've ever lived with a cat, then this book is for you ... In *My Life in a Cat House,* Cooper lovingly and humorously depicts the ups and downs of a life with cats and the ways in which they mimic human behavior and feelings. A fun read for all animal lovers."
—*New York Journal of Books*

"A literary fur fix for Homer fans!"
—*Catster* magazine

"As Gwen shares the joys, sorrows, laughter and tears of sharing her life with her cats, both past and present, you will find yourself nodding in recognition and perhaps remember the antics of a cat long gone. You may even gain a deeper understanding of your own feline companions."

—The Conscious Cat

"Gwen has the uncanny ability to touch our hearts with her gift of conveying thought-provoking and heart-stirring emotions...Gwen's writing is unpretentious, it's authentic, it's REAL. Whether like me you have nearly all of Gwen's books, or if this one is your first, you will delight in her descriptive, often hilarious and loving stories about her cats."

—Cat Chat with Caren and Cody

"There's something about Gwen Cooper's cat books that touch my heart like few others, and *My Life in a Cat House* is no exception. Whether you've enjoyed every one of Gwen's cat books or this is your first, snuggle up with a cat or two while you're reading. I guarantee with each turn of the page you'll pull them just a little bit closer as you realize just how empty your life would be without their unconditional love."

—Melissa's Mochas, Mysteries and Meows

"Gwen Cooper is the Queen of Cat Love—and in these fun and frisky stories, she perfectly captures all the reasons felines rule our hearts and our homes. No cat lover should be without this book, but more important, give it to the folks who haven't yet seen the light. At least they'll understand us better!"

—Sy Montgomery, bestselling author of *How to Be a Good Creature: A Memoir in Thirteen Animals*

"What a pleasure to read [Gwen Cooper's] beautiful stories, brimming with her cat-love and even more important her ability to get you to actually see her cats . . . You will want to see more and more. She can become your next obsession, as she has become mine!"

Praise for Love Saves the Day

Also by Gwen Cooper

The
PAWSOME!
Collection

*The Book of PAWSOME! Head Bonks,
Raspy Tongues & 101 Reasons Why Cats
Make Us So, So Happy*

and

*<u>YOU</u> are PAWSOME! 75 Reasons Why
Your Cats Love You, and Why Loving
Them Back Makes You a Better Human*

GWEN COOPER

Originally published in paperback in the United States by Interrobang Books as *The Book of PAWSOME! Head Bonks, Raspy Tongues, and 101 Reasons Why Cats Make Us So, So Happy* in 2020.

Originally published in paperback in the United States by Interrobang Books as *YOU are PAWSOME! 75 Reasons Why Your Cats Love You, and Why Loving Them Back Makes You a Better Human* in 2022.

Cooper, Gwen.
The PAWSOME! Collection
ISBN 979-8-9867722-7-1

Nonfiction; humor; pets

Illustrations by Jessica Rodrigue

Contents

PAWSOME!

HEAD BONKS, RASPY TONGUES, AND 101 REASONS WHY CATS MAKE US SO, SO HAPPY

GWEN COOPER

NEW YORK TIMES BESTSELLING AUTHOR OF HOMER'S ODYSSEY

Foreword

I t was back in mid-February of 2020—almost exactly one month to the day before the world began to shut down—when I was browsing through a bookstore and spotted a title that, despite its having been a big bestseller, I'd never heard of.

It was by someone named Neil Parischa and was called *The Book of Awesome: Snow Days, Bakery Air, Finding Money in Your Pocket, and Other Simple, Brilliant Things*. From a marketing perspective it was a brilliant title, insofar as I immediately and intuitively grasped what the book was about. And, just as immediately, I wondered, *Why isn't there a Book of PAWsome about cats?*

And so it was that this book was born.

There aren't any hard-and-fast rules governing either the specific entries or the lengths of those entries in this book, aside from my gut feeling that each entry is as long or short as it ought to be. The entries in the first section, however—which is dedicated to capturing the joy in specific moments *with* cats, as opposed to certain qualities that cats have—tend to be a bit shorter.

I also tried to avoid being too "explain-y" for the most part. There are plenty of books out there that will tell you the whys and where-fores about the ways in which cats behave, and I wasn't seeking to duplicate their efforts.

Last but not least, I also made a commitment to playing it straight. In other words, while this book is certainly (raspy) tongue-in-cheek, it's never sarcastic. Even when an entry seems to dwell on one of the very few alleged "negatives" of living with a cat—the way, for example, a cat will rip up toilet paper just when it's become *extremely* difficult to find—I, personally, am always more genuinely tickled than annoyed when my cats shred paper goods. And since it's something cats do that makes me laugh, I included it in the book.

Ultimately, what I hope is that you, too, will enjoy a good chuckle when you read these pages, and find a little of the joy in everyday things—and in every day we get to spend with our cats—that can sometimes seem elusive. I'm an incurable optimist, something I inherited from my grandmother, and I always do believe that, with our cats by our sides, better days lie ahead for all of us.

Optimism is also something I get from my cats, who never seem less than 100% certain that another bag of Greenies is waiting for them at the end of the rainbow...

PAWSOME!

Contents

Days of Heaven

*Those little moments of **PAWSOME!**
that cat lovers live for...*

When your cat is completely hidden under the bed...except for the little tail that's sticking out

"I f I can't see *you*, then you can't see *me*!"

PAWSOME!

When your cat pats you very gently with her paw to get your attention

C ats have a reputation for being "aloof" and "standoffish" creatures—and it may often seem as if that reputation is well
earned. But anybody who's lived with a cat knows that sometimes
they're actually quite desperate for human attention.

Not that *acting* desperate is in a cat's nature. Heavens no! Rather,
cats tend to prefer the subtle approach.

If it were another person trying to get your attention, they might
holler your name or shoot over a buzzing and intrusive text message.
An enthusiastic dog might bark and whine and jump at you until
you were forced to look up from your book, or perhaps relinquish a
morsel of food from your plate, as an act of simple self-preservation.

But cats are exquisitely courteous when they wish to be. A cat
who's hoping to draw your eyes from that book, or score a tempting
table tidbit, likely won't shriek or leap at you. Holding his desperate
impulses in check, your cat will instead very gently and respectfully
pat your shoulder or leg a few times with his velvety front paw (claws
retracted, of course) until you finally look his way. Almost as if he
were saying: "I'm *terribly* sorry, old chap, but if it wouldn't be *too*
much trouble to give me your attention for *just* a moment..."

It's the politeness of it that always kills me.

So terribly well-mannered. More than a little endearing. And
oh-so-very
PAWSOME!

When you wake up early on a Sunday morning to feed your cat and realize you can get back into bed for another two or three hours

Waking up in the mornings to a fuzzy, whiskered snout rubbing gently against your face is infinitely better than being jarred into the day by the grating buzzer of an alarm clock, as any cat lover will tell you.

The problem, however, and as the old saying goes, is that there's no snooze button on a hungry cat. If your cat is used to getting breakfast at 6:00 a.m. while you begin your mad scramble of showering, making up, and dressing before flying out the door for your workday commute, then 6:00 a.m. is when your cat will expect to be fed *every* morning—even on Sundays, the one day out of the whole week when you can lie about as late as you want to, like you were the Queen of England.

Still, there's something to be said for being awakened for breakfast of a Sunday morning by your impatient cat and then realizing—after your cat has been fed—that *you can get back into bed* and stay there for hours, blissfully inert. Maybe you catch some more Z's. Maybe you turn on your bedroom TV to that basic cable station that plays Sunday-morning reruns of your all-time favorite shows. Maybe you just wrap yourself up in your warm blanket, flip your pillow over to the cool side, and snuggle in, thinking: *This is the life!* Chances are your furry bestie will improve an already *purr*fect scenario by joining you for that excellent Sunday bonus nap, once her hunger has been sated.

The point is, you can spend an extra three or four idyllic hours in one of the best places in the whole world—your very own bed—re-awaken in plenty of time to throw on sweats and beat the Sunday-morning rush at your favorite pancake joint (having a semi-empty diner nearly all to yourself on a Sunday morning is *soooooo great!*), and *still* have an entire lazy Sunday in front of you when you finally emerge, happily stuffed with pancakes, the sweetness of melted butter and maple syrup warm on your tongue.

If it weren't for your cat, you would have slept all the way through those golden hours of self-indulgence. You would have missed out on that fifth re-viewing of Season 3 *Mad Men* from the comfort of your bed, followed by bacon and flapjacks. You would have woken up hours later, bleary-eyed and bewildered because you blew right past your usual wake-up time. You would've opened your eyes to full, disorienting daylight, along with the alarmed feeling of *Did I oversleep?!!?* before remembering that it's Sunday—an entire glorious day off that, sadly, is now already halfway gone, before you got a chance to bask fully in Sunday-morning delights.

But that didn't happen to you. *You*, you lucky human, were able to add a joyfully languid three or four hours onto your already leisurely Sunday, and it's all thanks to the purring bundle of love cuddled up next to you in the bed.

And that's **PAWSOME!**

When cats wiggle their butts before they pounce

Nobody's sure why cats wiggle their butts before they pounce. Theories range from it being a type of kitty calisthenics (to warm up their muscles before a leap), a way of getting a firmer foothold before launching an attack, a method of adding greater momentum to a jump, and possibly a way of focusing a cat's attention.

Then again, why ask why? It's hilarious, it's hella fun to watch, and ultimately we have only one thing to say on the subject:

Shake it like a Polaroid picture, kitty!

PAWSOME!

When you bring home a new kind of cat food, and your cat actually likes it!

We've all been there. Maybe the pet store has run out of Mr. Whiskers' favorite flavor of food. Maybe the manufacturer discontinued it. Maybe there's a food that your cat absolutely *loved* as recently as yesterday, but today when you put it down, Mr. Whiskers not only refused to touch it, he gave you the sulky stink-eye all afternoon.

(*But you loved it YESTERDAY!* A cry from the cat lover's very soul.)

The only thing you can ever really know for sure about cats is that their decision-making process is ultimately unknowable—which means you're pretty much just groping in the dark on those occasions when circumstances force you to seek out a new flavor of food for your kitty's consumption. *He always enjoys tuna...I guess that's close enough to mackerel to give it a shot?*

Sadly, when you finally get that new brand or flavor of food home—and set it before your finicky feline as anxiously as an aspiring singer auditioning for an industry legend—your only likely reward for all the time and careful deliberation you've invested will be an upturned nose and the sight of your cat's backside stalking away.

But, every so often, the stars align just right—and Mr. Whiskers actually *likes* the new flavor! The little mound of food in the dish gets smaller and smaller until there's nothing but empty dish left—and beside that empty dish Mr. Whiskers is now luxuriously and elaborately cleaning his snout, which is the feline equivalent of lighting a cigarette and unbuckling your belt following a thoroughly satisfying meal.

You did it! Yippee!!!!!!!!!!!!

Now you don't have a thing in the world to worry about—at least, not until the pet store runs out of this food, as well.

PAWSOME!

When you buy your cat a new toy, and she actually plays with it!

C at toys are a suckers' game. You stand in front of that colorful display in the pet store full of hope and enthusiasm, trying to determine exactly which of the bouncing, buzzing, rolling, springing, or airborne gizmos in front of you will best tempt your opinionated tabby into cavorting delightfully around the living room for, perhaps, as long as five completely entertaining minutes. *This time, I've done it*, you think, as you walk out of the pet store clutching a shopping bag filled with dollar-ninety-eight treasures. You're as proud as a Viking carrying sacks of gold and other spoils of battle back to your homeland and lady-love, ready to throw them at her feet as you assure yourself that, *This time I've found at least one toy that Fluffy will love!*

When you arrive home with that pet-store bag in your hand, however, you realize just how futile those hopes were. Fussy little Fluffy is certainly very interested in the *bag* that the toy came in. Ah, the endless possibilities of a bag! A cat can sleep on top of a bag, or turn a bag into a just-her-size makeshift cave, or chew a bag to bits, leaving a trail of itty-bitty bag scraps strewn on the floor all around her.

But the toy itself—this object to which you've affixed your dreams of glory, and on the selection of which you expended at least a good fifteen or twenty minutes—is sniffed at for perhaps all of four seconds. Then it's ignored completely, left to make its slow, sad voyage to the toy graveyard that accumulates in one corner of the living room until it's time for spring cleaning, when all the unsuccessful toys are looked at one last time (farewell, rubber ball with feather attached; we hardly knew ye, cotton-stuffed striped goldfish) before being tossed out with the trash.

Still, statisticians tell us that, on a long enough timeline, anything that *can* happen *will* happen. So, every so often, through the sheer law of averages, you hit by chance upon a toy that your cat actually *likes*! The glory of it! Your cat sniffs at the toy, perhaps suspiciously at first. (*What fresh hell is this?*) But then suspicion gives way to curiosity, curiosity turns to playfulness, and finally—miracle of miracles!—Fluffy cavorts, she capers, she leaps and dips and spins with glee. She races across the room to fling herself on the couch, dragging her brand-new and already beloved toy with her, where she proceeds to claw it, bite it, maul it, and eventually nap right next to it for the next several hours at least.

YOU DID IT!!!

For perhaps an entire afternoon—maybe even as long as one whole week!—Fluffy is fascinated with the goods that the gods...or, y'know, *you*...have seen fit to provide her. And *you* get to strut proudly and triumphantly around the house like the conquering hero you are.

PAWSOME!

When you see your cat sleeping in a pool of sunlight

Every so often, on a sunny spring day, when I walk into a room to find one of my cats sprawled out and blissfully asleep in a pool of sunlight streaming through the window—every strand of fur illuminated and glowing like a halo—a feeling of pure peacefulness cups my heart.

Do you know that feeling?

And, if it's a black cat, sometimes you even catch a glimpse of a chocolate-brown or tabby-striped undercoat that remains hidden most of the time.

So beautiful. So, so **PAWSOME.**

When your cat gives you the heavy-lidded look of, "I love you soooooo much..."

T here are "experts" who say that, because cats have fewer muscles around their eyes than dogs do, their faces are therefore less expressive.

Don't believe it for one second.

Anyone who's lived with a cat for any length of time is familiar with *the look*. You know the one I'm talking about: that eyes-half-closed gaze of *purr*fect adoration your cat will sometimes bestow upon you—when he half-wakes from a particularly excellent nap to the gentle touch of your hand; when your fingers have managed to find that one spot to scratch behind his ears that's *juuuuuuuuuuust* right; when you're standing in the kitchen chopping vegetables and, for no particular reason, he comes in to stand beside you, flicks his tail around your lower leg, and turns his head to gaze up at you with his whole heart in his eyes.

You might only see that gaze in your cat's eyes for a moment—but it's a moment that will stick with you for the rest of your life.

PAWSOME!

When your cat stands on his hind legs like a meerkat

S o doofy. So adorable. So unbelievably...

PAWSOME!

When your cat gets into a life-and-death battle with a piece of lint

O ne of the greatest things about cats is that they have such vivid imaginations.

Sadly, it's impossible for cats to tell us the stories they make up in their heads. Still, we have ample evidence of their epic fantasy lives on full display before our very eyes.

It's evident, for example, when your cat *veeeeeeeeeery* slowly sneaks up on some inanimate toy that, y'know, can't actually *see* her coming. It's clear that, in your cat's mind, however, that harmless-looking plaything is actually a mortal foe—one crafty enough that your intrepid feline has to execute a careful stealth attack to give herself the tactical advantage of surprise. *Well, well, Dr. Felt-Mouse...so we meet again...*

But never is this abundant imagination on greater display than when your cat is embroiled in a rolled-on-her-back, bunny-feet-kicking, *battle royale* to the death with...well, it's hard to tell. A shifty-looking gnat? A piece of lint that got a little too mouthy?

Watching your cat stage an epic mêlée with nothing in particular is a wonderful and constant reminder of what it felt like to be a kid—a harkening back to days when you didn't need much more to conjure up entertainment than your own imagination.

PAWSOME!

When your cat puts two paws on your chest and very sweetly asks to be petted

C ats take a lot of ribbing for being stubborn, opinionated, temperamental, aloof, lazy, erratic, and more.

(Honestly, though, who among *isn't* most of those things sometimes? For me, personally, it's a good day when I'm only one or two of them.)

But the closely guarded secret known only to cat lovers is that cats can, more often than not, be such incredible little *loves*. Like when you're just hanging out on the couch watching TV or reading a book, and your cat suddenly springs up next to you, rises up on her hind legs, then very gently (and very sweetly) places her two front paws on your chest in an unmistakable *please pet me* request.

Maybe she even raises her head to touch her little nose to yours.

There's only word in the English language capable of describing the utter, heart-melting adorableness of such moments: *Awwwwwwwwwwwww...*

Actually, make that two:

PAWSOME!

When your cat "follows" you from the front

It's incredibly endearing when your cat is so enamored of your presence that he eagerly follows you from room to room.

But what's even cuter than *that* is when your cat is just so gosh-darn thrilled to be with you that he's too giddy and impatient to actually wait while you go from one room to the other. Instead, he races out ahead of you—but remains close enough to turn his head back from time to time to make sure you're still right there with him. And his ears will turn back, too—just to keep extra tabs on you.

It's as if every inch of his body is crying out, *Let's hurry up and get there so we can cuddle already!*

My cat Homer used to do this all the time.

It's thoroughly adorable, completely loving, and absolutely **PAWSOME!**

When you hug your cat and he smells like cookies

T his may be too specific to apply to most cats, because it's something I've personally experienced with only one of the cats I've lived with. But my cat Homer sometimes smelled like cookies. Or, to be precise, the back of his neck occasionally gave off a very distinct aroma that always made me think of my childhood, and of afternoons at the kitchen table with a plate of warm cinnamon cookies and a tall, cool glass of milk to dunk them in.

Homer was only a tiny kitten the first time when, while cuddling him, I caught a whiff of cinnamon and milk. I wondered briefly if I might be experiencing some sort of apoplexy, because I'd read somewhere that smelling oranges, for example, when there weren't any oranges around might be a sign you were having a stroke. But over the next few months I noticed that same comforting smell a few more times when I picked Homer up or affectionately buried my nose in the scruff of his neck, which seemed to argue against the "it's a stroke" theory.

For years, I assumed that a tendency to smell like baked goods was unique to Homer—an additional special quality in a cat already special in so many ways. I wasn't even entirely sure that it wasn't all in my head, since I usually noticed the fragrance most strongly when I was feeling down or in especial need of Homer's comfort.

But nearly two decades later, while working on a book about him, I described in some detail this particularly endearing trait, and my cat-loving copy editor dropped in the following note while reviewing the manuscript: *I know exactly what you mean! My Jasper smelled just like my mom's vanilla coconut cookies!*

So there you have it. If I were a betting woman (full disclosure: I find gambling to be intensely stressful), I'd wager that somewhere out there are even more cat ladies and cat dudes who can report similar phenomena. Lovers of cookie-smelling cats, unite!

One of my favorite network shows in recent years was *The Good Place*, an NBC sitcom about a woman who winds up in Heaven by mistake. In one episode, it's explained that Heaven smells different for everyone, depending on what their favorite smell was while they were alive on Earth.

If that turns out to be true, then I know exactly what Heaven's fragrance will be for me. When the pearly gates open wide to take me in, wafting through them will be the aroma of a little blind, black cat—a cat who somehow, mysteriously, smelled just like fresh cinnamon cookies right out of the oven...

PAWSOME!

When your cat slow-blinks at you

No less a person than world-famous cat behaviorist Jackson Galaxy has said that when a cat slowly blinks at you—not just a regular blink, but a very deliberate and languid slow-blink of the eyes—it's essentially a feline way of saying, "I love you."

Cats are predators, but they're also prey, and are therefore reluctant to show their vulnerabilities. So when your cat slow-blinks at you, he's basically letting you know that he feels very safe and comfortable in your presence—so safe and comfortable, in fact, that he's able to close his eyes for a moment, knowing that you can be completely trusted.

Cats aren't exactly known for their blind faith in others, and the number of people (or other cats) that the typical feline trusts completely is usually very, *very* small. So having successfully earned the trust of a cat isn't an accomplishment that anybody should take lightly.

In fact, it's pretty **PAWSOME!**

When your cat sleeps with one paw over her eyes

E verybody has their own opinion as to which of a cat's sleeping positions is the absolute cutest. And while there's a great deal to be said for Sprawled On Back With Tummy Showing, or Curled Up In Ball With Tail Covering Nose, for my money I'll take Paw Over Eyes every day of the week and twice on Sunday.

Usually a cat with her paw over her eyes will be partially rolled onto her side, which means you still get to see a good bit of mushy tummy—although, granted, not all of it. But what you lose in belly fluff, you more than make up for in paw. Cats' velvety-soft little paws are a great deal of their charm, but rarely do you get the unobstructed view of teeny-tiny toe beans that the Paw Over Eyes sleeping position offers.

And there's something so touching and almost *human* about a cat sleeping with one paw flung casually across her face. I'm not necessarily an adherent to the "cats are little people in fur suits" school of thought but, at such moments, I'm halfway there.

Ultimately, though, it probably pays not to try to dissect the cuteness of it too much. Rather, we should simply accept these gifts of adorableness wherever we find them, and agree that it's indisputably **PAWSOME!**

When your cat plays with running water

C ats have a general aversion to water that's well known even among people who know little else about cats. And, indeed, it's tough to imagine a sadder sight than that of a bedraggled, soaking wet, and thoroughly discomfited cat (poor little thing!).

But while most cats (with a few breed exceptions) might not like *immersing* themselves in water—and while the typical cat on a wet-food diet might even avoid drinking too much water—that doesn't mean they have no interest in liquids whatsoever.

Your cat might be fascinated with watching water run out of a flushing toilet bowl, for example. Or she might show a lively interest in running water straight from the tap.

Even some cats who are water-shy for the most part will find it fascinating when it's running out of a faucet. Experts say that a cat might prefer drinking from a tap to drinking from a bowl because running tap water is fresher and more oxygenated. Regardless of the reason, seeing that sideways kitty head tilt—a bid to give their little pink tongue a better lapping angle—never fails to tickle me.

Even cuter is the way some cats will "wash" their paws in running water—although, here again, experts will chime in to sathe reason they're doing that is to filter the water through the strands of fur on their paws. So, nature's answer to a Brita, basically, rather than an attempt to mimic human habits of hand sanitation.

Nevertheless, it's still *paws*itively adorable!

Pro tip: A great way to get your cat to drink more water (most cats would benefit from being a tad more hydrated) while also upping your amusement factor is to buy your pampered puss his very own cat fountain. You can find tons of reasonably priced options on Amazon or at your local pet store.

Then just plug that bad boy in, fill it with water, and immerse yourself in the **PAWSOME!**

When your cat tries to squeeze into a too-small cardboard box

You will never love anything the way your cat loves a cardboard box.

He'll love it whether it's been dyed deep crimson or remains plain cardboard brown; whether it has fancy writing on its sides or no design at all; whether it's brand spanking new or has been lying around in an attic for the better part of a decade.

And he'll love that box even if it's way too big or too small to provide maximum kitty comfort.

Watching a cat trying to squeeze himself into a cardboard box that's far, *far* too small is *far* more entertaining than it should be. It's like watching a mean-spirited society matron at Saks trying to shove a size-ten foot into a size-six pump. It's like watching all those circus clowns who come pouring out of the tiny clown car trying to stuff themselves back into it.

Not too many things will make you laugh harder, in other words—and if it's been too long since you've seen this particular bit of comedy gold play out in your own home, then maybe it's time to order a book from Amazon post-haste, just so you can get one of those little boxes they send out single books in.

When your book arrives, you know exactly what to do: Remove book from box, set that itty-bitty box out on your living room floor, call your cat over...

And let the **PAWSOME** begin!

When your cat chases shimmers and sunbeams up the wall

I t's an odd quirk of the human/feline relationship that the more a cat stares at something with plainly murderous intent, the more adorable we find said cat to be.

I'm not talking about songbirds or pet gerbils or anything that's, y'know, *alive*. I mean when we see a cat giving the all-pupils Murder Look to a Christmas-tree ornament, or the ballerina figurine atop a little girl's birthday cake, or even a small stuffed animal.

Harmless things. *Pretty* things. And yet, the prettier and more harmless the prospective "victim" is in this scenario, the more we coo delightedly as we watch Bootsie hunker down and prepare to leap in full KILL-CRUSH-DESTROY mode at a festive scrap of giftwrap paper. *Who's mommy's little predator? Who's my fuzzy-wuzzy wizzle killer?*

Among the very prettiest things your cat will do her absolute level best to murder for your amusement are the shimmers that fall through windows onto walls and floors on a sunny day. They might be rainbow-colored and cast by a prism hanging from a window frame, or simply the ghostly-white result of light striking a reflective surface at a certain angle—a glass coffee table, perhaps, or the face of your cell phone.

I will freely confess that, in my house, the light shimmers are often created on purpose by me—deliberately toggling my glasses back and forth in the light—just because it's so much *fun* to watch my cats track its progress up the wall, across the ceiling, and back down an opposite wall. (Watching both their heads crane up at identical angles and move from left to right in perfect sync—like two little sunflowers—kills me every single time.) Their eyes become *enormous*, and they crouch down low on their hind legs until the tension is nearly unbearable—at which point they spring directly at the wall and the light shimmer they've been tracking, only to discover that their paws are empty.

My cats have been doing this for years now, and the fact that they've never once succeeded in pinning down a light shimmer and killing the heck out of it doesn't seem to have taken one particle of fun out of the game for them—or made it one iota less entertaining for me to watch.

The light shimmer is an illusion, of course. There's no possible way for them ever to catch it. Nevertheless, their hope that maybe *this* time they'll finally get their paws around that elusive prize burns as bright as the sun that casts the shimmers they chase.

In this, my cats display an optimism well worth emulating.
PAWSOME!

When your cat leans hard into your hand during a scritching session

D o cats enjoy receiving head scritches more than we like giving them? Impossible to say!

If you're a cat lover, though, then you know that great moment—when you're scritching your cat behind the ears or under the chin, and then your cat leans his head with more and more weight into your palm, his eyes completely closed, a look of utter bliss etched on his face, and you not only hear but actually *feel* the rumbling sound of his purr as it ripples across the flesh of your hand...

PAWSOME!

When it's like your cat can read your mind

O kay, so mind-reading isn't really a real thing, much less a technique your kitty has actually mastered (preternaturally bright though he may be). You will almost certainly never go to the fortune-telling booth at a county fair and find a cat in full turban, sitting behind a crystal ball among billowing clouds of incense, ready to tell you the future. (*I see a white cat in your life...I see you giving him a can of tuna when you get home...*)

Even so, you'd be hard-pressed to find a cat lover who wouldn't swear up and down that cats have a knack for knowing when their humans are feeling blue and need some extra cuddling, or feeling a bit irritated and in need of some alone time, or simply in the mood to snuggle up under the covers with an old movie and a warm, purring feline for company.

And that's not even counting the way cats seem to know, somehow, the difference between when you're taking out the can opener for a can of soup versus a can of tuna (*tuna!!!*). I'll walk back and forth across the living room a dozen times without my cats so much as batting an eyelash—but when I get up the thirteenth time, planning to "surprise" them with a treat from the Greenies bag, somehow they've already beaten me to the drawer in the end table where the Greenies are kept.

First things first, cats actually *do* have some legit superpowers: a cat's sense of smell is about fourteen times stronger than a human's, they can hear sounds three times higher than what a human can hear, and their vision (particularly at night) is far superior to ours. Not to mention that cats are basically *purr*fectly designed predators, which gives them extraordinary observation skills. You may not realize that you have your gaze turned slightly in the direction of the treats drawer when you're heading over to it—or that the cabinet holding your cans of tuna sounds *juuuuuuust* slightly different when it's opened than the cabinet where you keep your soup—but these are the kinds of things your cats will definitely make note of.

And, of course, if you're feeling sad, or anxious, or giddy and ebullient, or if you're off your usual game in some other significant way, there will be all kinds of subtle changes in the way you sit, the way you hold your body, the timbre of your voice, the size of your pupils—even, according to some studies, in the way you smell. All these nearly imperceptible things (imperceptible to humans, that is) combine to give your perceptive puss a pretty accurate gauge of what your state of mind is at any given moment.

Not that any of this explains the incredible empathy your cat is capable of on those days when you do need that extra round of purrs and cuddles to keep you going.

That's just his special gift—because your cat is
PAWSOME.

When your cat mushes his little face right up against yours

There you are, reading a book, oblivious to whatever is going on around you, when your cat approaches silently on little padded paws and doesn't just give you a "what's up?" head bonk, but actually presses his entire face to your forehead in the feline equivalent of a warm, spontaneous hug.

Or maybe you're nose to nose with him, gently scratching him behind the ears, when—after touching his nose lightly to yours—he mushes his face against your face and holds it there for a moment.

Sure, there's some "scent marking" involved here. But I think it's more than that. Cats don't have many of the same affectionate gestures at their disposal that we have at ours, after all. They can't pick us up or cuddle us in *their* laps or scritch us behind *our* ears or open a cabinet to dispense some much-loved treat to us. (Insofar as some cats *can* open cabinets and dispense treats, they typically only do so for themselves.)

But one thing your cat absolutely can do is press his face to yours and hold it there for a long moment, as if to say, *You know I love you more than anyone else in the whole world, right?*

And it's one of the greatest moments of **PAWSOME** that cat lovers live for...

When your cat waits anxiously outside the shower for you

I can only speak for myself, of course, but I get a kick out of those times when I see one or more of my cats pacing anxiously next to the shower while I'm in there.

Whether it's because they're panicked at the thought of me—*the human who feeds them,* for god's sake!—being exposed to all that water (to be trapped in an enclosed space, unable to escape the cascade of water that pours down on you relentlessly, is the stuff of kitty night terrors); or simply because I've gone to just about the only place in the house where they can't follow, I'll never know.

The one thing that's clear is that they do not like it. At. All.

Generally I'm the one worrying about the health, happiness, and wellbeing of my cats, rather than the other way around. But, still...knowing that they love me enough to worry about *my* health and wellbeing sometimes?

There's no denying...it's pretty **PAWSOME**!

When, immediately upon seeing you, your cat's tail stands straight up and vibrates

W hen was the last time you saw a person whom you see every single day, and they burst out with an exuberant, "OH MY GOD!!! I'M SOOOOOOO THRILLED TO SEE YOU!!!" Because that's exactly what your cat is saying when his tail sticks straight up in the air and vibrates.

And it's *the best.*

To those uninitiated into the mysteries of feline communication, it all seems simple: Dogs' tails wag when they're happy, cats' tails wag when they're *un*happy, and that's all there is to know.

But, like strangers in a strange land who will never grasp more than the rudiments of a foreign language, there's a whole lot of nuance that such people are missing out on. Cats' tails are finely tuned communication devices, able to convey a full range of moods and sentiments of which "happy" and "unhappy" are barely the tip of the iceberg.

A tail that's curved like a question mark, for example, means that it's time for you to dig out Da Bird or a favorite catnip toy, because your cat is in a playful mood. If his tail is swishing slowly from side to side, he's concentrating on something intently (possibly contemplating the best and most efficient way to persuade you to spontaneously crack open that bag of treats). When your cat gently curls his tail around you—or another cat—that's basically the equivalent of a person slinging an arm over your shoulders in a warm half-hug and saying, *Hello, friend.*

A whipping tail means that something is bothering your cat mightily and is a definite sign to any observer that backing up a foot or two (or five) is probably a wise move. A low-hanging tail can also be a sign of aggression, and a puffed-up tail like a bottle brush means that your cat is trying to look bigger than his actual size and indicates Aggression with a capital "A." (It may seem as if cats have a *lot* of ways of expressing aggression—but, considering how many times I've heard someone say, *I was just petting him and he bit me out of nowhere!* maybe they need a few more.)

But when a cat's tail sticks straight up, that means he's happy. And when his tail sticks straight up and *vibrates*—that, my feline-loving friend, is a veritable love song of enthusiasm. That's your cat's way of saying: *I love you, love you, LOVE you!!!*

We all have a tendency to take for granted the people we see every day—even the people we love the most. We don't always act as happy—or remember even to *feel* as happy—as we should when our eyes happen to fall on a beloved face. And the people who love us the most in return don't necessarily light up every time we walk into a room—especially when we've spent the last decade or two walking in and out of the exact same room to see and be seen by the exact same face.

But when your cat's tail stands straight up and does its happy dance, that's when you know there's at least one soul in this whole wide world who's downright *ecstatic* at the knowledge that a) you exist, and b) you're right here, right now, where he can gaze upon you in all your glory.

And it doesn't get any more **PAWSOME** than that.

When your cat falls asleep in your lap

L et's agree that, of all God's creatures large and small whom we humans have domesticated or been domesticated by over the millennia of our existence here on planet Earth—the dog, the horse, the bunny, to name but a few—the housecat is the most consistently and perfectly lap-sized of them all. It's the rare adult cat who's *so* small as to slip right through your lap the way a ferret would, for example. And even a full-grown Maine Coon will come much, *much* closer to fitting snugly within lap-sized confines than, say, a Great Dane.

Let's also agree that, among the numerous transcendent pleasures that come as part and parcel of living with a cat, among the most transcendent of them all is when your cat falls asleep in your lap.

Is there any greater bliss?

First and foremost, cats just look so darn *good* when they're sleeping. Maybe your cat likes to curl up in a tight ball with her tail wrapped snugly around her little nose. Maybe she sprawls out on her side, or (even better!) on her *back* with all four paws in the air, her temptingly squeezable tummy on full display. Perhaps she tucks her paws beneath her in a classic "cat as loaf of bread" pose. Whatever the sleeping position *du jour* happens to be, nothing will ever beat a lap-side view of the proceedings—an up-close and *purr*sonal perspective from which you can even see the gentle, back-and-forth sway of your kitty's whiskers as she breathes in and out.

And then there's the incomparable joy of having a semi-wild creature trust you enough to fall asleep in your lap. No cat is ever more than partially tamed at best, and cats have probably domesticated *us* at least as much as we've domesticated them. And so, in addition to the warmth and comfort all that physical closeness brings, there's also an undeniable hint of glamor—a whisper of mystery—when your cat steals softly across your legs. Nothing will ever make you feel more *chosen*. You've been selected and set apart from the great masses of humanity because of some exceptional quality you possess—a quality that's perfectly visible to your cat, even if not to yourself.

It's a moment of grace. Almost as if some wild creature had crept out of the jungle to lay his head in your lap, or some exotic bird of paradise had descended from the heavens for a fleeting moment and gently kissed you on the cheek.

If you're anything like me, the feeling of utter peace that settles over you when your cat curls or sprawls across your lap is of a deeper and more durable register than anything a paid expert in relaxation exercises or guided meditation could ever help you achieve.

Which makes it completely unsurprising that people who live with cats are forty percent less likely to suffer from heart attacks or other stress-related illnesses.

PAWSOME!

When your cat's whiskers tickle your face

A cat's whiskers are just about the cattiest cat thing going. While lots of other animals have them, we typically associate whiskers with cats—in fact, we call catfish "catfish" specifically because they, like cats, have whiskers. (Although technically what catfish have are called "barbels.")

I love seeing the profusion of my cats' whiskers—the super-long lengths of my chubbier kitty's set (whiskers typically grow out a tad wider than a cat's body, so, in the case of my husky boy, they have a lot of ground to cover!) and the more delicate span of my slender cat's. I love the abundance of them, sprouting from my cats' cheeks and above their eyes like the scraggly eyebrows and bushy beard of a very wise old man. I love watching my cats contentedly clean their whiskers following a meal, and the way they turn a shimmering, iridescent silver in the sun.

Best of all, though, is when I'm lying in bed or on the couch with my eyes closed and my cat decides to join me—and a millisecond or two before I feel the warmth of his body or the softness of his fur, I'll feel the shivery tickle of his whiskers brushing against my cheek, like wispy little heralds sent ahead to announce their master's imminent arrival.

And, in that millisecond, I know that purrs and cuddles are in my very near future.

PAWSOME!

When you fall asleep to the sound of your cat's purr

It's something every cat has, although no two are ever exactly alike. It has magical healing properties—including the ability to promote bone growth and repair and to reduce high blood pressure. We associate it with cats, although it's a trait they share with hyenas, mongooses, raccoons, guinea pigs, genets, and civets. And even though you can't actually see it, it's something every cat lover would recognize anywhere—even in the dark.

I'm speaking, of course, about a cat's purr.

Of all the varied and glorious things there are to love about cats (I say this as someone who's compiled a whole book about them!), the purr is one of my absolute favorite things of all—and I'm guessing the same is true for you. For one thing, there are so few sounds in life that also bring with them such a pleasurable tactile *feeling* as a cat's purr. (I guess, technically, I can also feel it when my neighbor's got the bass on his stereo cranked up way too loud—but I wouldn't actually call that "pleasurable.")

And while it's true that cats will sometimes purr to "self soothe" during times of stress, it's a sound most often associated with *purr*-fect satisfaction. When you're the one causing your cat's bliss—by the well-timed application of a back scratch or ear rub, for example—hearing and feeling that deep rumble of *purr* happiness emanate from your contented kitty is the best of all possible rewards.

I love hearing my cats' purrs first thing in the morning when we've all just woken up. I love hearing purrs when I stoop to give my cats a quick scritch upon returning home after several hours away. I love hearing them as my cats are digging into their breakfast. I love it when I'm watching TV or reading a book with a cat curled up in my lap or right next to me on the couch, snoozing and purring as I stroke their back without even thinking about it.

There's never a bad time to hear the happy purrs of a happy cat, and no good thing that a good loud purr couldn't make just a wee bit better. Still, my absolute favorite of all favorite times to hear my cats' purrs is in bed at night as I'm falling asleep with one (or more!) or them right next to me. I love falling asleep to the sound of my cats' purrs more than I love falling asleep to the sounds of my favorite classical music, or a white noise machine, or the sounds of waves crashing on the shore during a beach vacation.

I think I even love falling asleep to the sound of my cats' purrs more than (don't tell him I said this!) the sound of my husband breathing next to me.

Don't get me wrong—I *love* falling asleep with my husband next to me! But, even at its deepest and most soothing, my husband's breathing doesn't have that same deep, soothing, **PAWSOME** rumble that my cats' purrs do...

Why Ask Why?

*Cats are **PAWSOME!** because...*

Cats are insanely adorable

I t's a fact so obvious that it almost goes without saying—but this book couldn't possibly be complete if it weren't stated at least once, clearly and for the record.

Your cat is adorable.

Seriously. Like, *insanely* adorable.

Those little paws, that tiny nose, those great big eyes...

And that belly! That glorious, fluffy, mushy little kitty belly!

It's enough to drive an otherwise sane and sober adult to helpless, babbling lunacy.

PAWSOME!

Cats' ears tell you how they're feeling

HAPPY

ANGRY

FRIGHTENED

PLAYFUL

CONTENT

PAWSOME!

Cats don't care about math

T rue story: I was just about finished with this book, and was getting ready to put it to bed, as we say in the biz, when—upon doing my final sweep for errors—I realized something awful:

I'd only written 100 entries; and, of course, this book's subtitle has promised *you*, dear reader, 101.

Fortunately, I had quite a few backups—there being far, *far* more than a mere 101 things to love about cats. As I was reading through them, though, trying to figure out which would be my last-minute addition, it occurred to me that one of the very best things about cats is that they would surely agree, if they could be made to understand the question, that math is basically a stupid waste of time anyway—unless you're a) an accountant, b) a literal rocket scientist, or c) trying to figure out exactly how much you'll save at a 50% off sale.

Amirite?

It's not just that cats *can't* do math. It's that if you waved a magic wand and gave them the ability to perform complex equations, they'd still make the entirely sensible decision to spend most of their time snoozing, daydreaming, looking out the window, and chasing sunbeams across the floor.

Quibbling over the very minor difference between 100 and 101 be damned.

Although I will say that my cats do seem to have the uncanny ability to figure out when I've accidentally given one of them more Pounce treats than the other.

PAWSOME!

Loving cats makes you smarter

B right as you are, you probably already knew this.

It may seem intuitively obvious that people who love cats tend to prize certain *purr*sonality traits—traits they're also likely to exhibit themselves. Introversion, sure, but also nonconformity (has your cat ever done *anything* just because you told her to?), open-mindedness (see above), and intelligence (cats manage to cozen us into feeding them despite apparently not giving a tinker's darn for what we want *them* to do—so obviously they've got something figured out). This stands opposed to the extroversion, conformity, and obedience that dog lovers seek in their own companions.

And now there's science to prove it. A 2010 study by Bristol University in the UK found that cat owners were likelier to have college and post-graduate degrees than dog owners (or any other kind of pet owner, for that matter), and a 2014 study by Carroll University in the U.S. backs that up. The U.S. study also showed that cat owners consistently score higher on intelligence tests than dog owners.

It should come as no surprise, therefore, that loving cats aligns you with some of the best and brightest figures in history—including Abraham Lincoln, Mark Twain, all three Bronte sisters, Charles Baudelaire, Ernest Hemingway, John Lennon, T.S. Eliot, William S. Burroughs, Catherine the Great, Marlon Brando, Freddie Mercury,

Neil Gaiman, Florence Nightingale, Stephen King, Jean Cocteau, Jean Paul Sartre, and Sir Isaac Newton.

There's no disputing it: Your love of cats practically assures your status as a certifiable genius.

PAWSOME!

Cats shower you with surprise gifts just because they think you're awesome

O ne of the very great joys in life is receiving gifts. Unfortunately, gift-giving occasions come around all too infrequently—and too often with disappointing results. (Show of hands if your junk drawer contains no fewer than five gift cards entitling you to $25 worth of merchandise in some store you've never spent so much as $1 in.)

And even assuming you're one of the lucky few who can count on opening a delightful box of Just What You Wanted on Christmas or birthdays, how long has it been since someone surprised you with a thoughtful present given to commemorate nothing in particular? When was the last time somebody handed you a gift-wrapped box on a random Tuesday and said, *I'm giving you this present just because I think you rock*?

Do you have to think back more than ten years to answer that question? Or is the answer maybe, just maybe, *never*?

If you live with a cat, I'm guessing your answer is more like, *A surprise gift? Why, I got one only last week!* And that's because cats *adore* bringing their humans considerate little love tokens for no other reason than to tell us, as clearly as if they'd said it in words, *Hey, you—you're WONDERFUL.*

True, our cats will rarely bring us something we would have picked out for ourselves. Cats, after all, are working within certain insurmountable limitations, such as not having charge accounts or access to Amazon Prime delivery. Also, a cat's worldview will differ in fundamental ways from a human's, tending to veer more toward the practical. Sparkly baubles are all well and good, and certainly fun to play with if they happen to dangle temptingly off the side of a dresser. But something you can *eat*—now *that's* solid gold, baby!

Which is why your felicitous feline will considerately place a small mouse or songbird—or, in the case of my own strictly indoor cats, plastic-and-felt reproductions of same—on your pillow, instead of a diamond bracelet or silk Hermés scarf.

But it's the thought that counts, and the thought in this case contains just as much downright, true-blue love as if it really were diamonds or silk. That fake mouse or disturbingly real songbird {{*shudder*}} is your cat's way of letting you know that he was thinking about you for no darn reason other than the fact that *you*—yes, *you*—are so indescribably marvelous that he can't help but think about you All. The. Time.

Who could put a price tag on that?

I once read somewhere that the "real" reason cats leave their humans gifts is because they think we're incompetent hunters who wouldn't be able to fend for ourselves without their help. But, with all due respect to Science, I think that's a load of hooey. Cats are smart creatures, and wicked observant, and they're perfectly capable of seeing us feed ourselves—and also feed them—and putting two and two together to conclude that, however sorry and colorless our lives might be without them, we certainly wouldn't starve.

So accept this gesture of love from your adoring kitty companion, icky though it may occasionally be, for exactly what it is: a concrete testament to the profound and timeless wonder that is *you*—the single greatest human out of all the humans on the face of the earth, in your cat's considered opinion—given for no other reason except that you're simply the kind of amazing person who deserves to be showered with gifts, nonstop.

PAWSOME!

Cats are yoga masters

A nd you don't even have to pay to attend their "classes."

Morning Salutation

Kitten Pose

Half Lotus

Full Lotus

Plank

The Pounce

PAWSOME!

Cats turn sick-days into fun-days

There you are—sore throat, stuffy nose, a bottle of Robitussin clutched in one clammy hand, and a trashcan overflowing with wadded up Kleenex next to the bed. Sure, you've got the day off from work, and that new Stephen King you've been wanting to dive into is waiting on the nightstand.

Still, you aren't exactly having fun.

You aren't, that is, unless you're lucky enough to share your home with a cat. Because in *that* scenario, despite being down with a head cold, you're also blissfully warm and comfortably ensconced beneath the covers with a furry buddy snoozing right beside you. You're hanging out with a four-legged *fur*iend who's practically giddy with infectious joy that you're home from work today. In the middle of the week! And even though it's well past noon, *you're still in bed!*

It's like Christmas came early!

So thrilled is your kitty with this unhoped-for bonus bed time, he won't leave your side all day—no matter how red and runny your nose gets or how loudly you cough. He'll stick around long after even the most devoted spouse has headed downstairs to get on with their own phlegm-free day.

And if you want to watch *Golden Girls* reruns for the thousandth time, just because it's the one silly thing that always makes you feel better no matter how sick you are, your cat will *totally* not make fun of your choice. In fact, his ecstatic purrs as he cuddles up next to you will add a delightful harmonic accompaniment to the comedy stylings of Betty White, et al.

Bonus benefit: Your cat's purrs vibrate at just the right frequency (between 25 and 150 Hertz) to help ease breathing difficulties and promote faster healing.

PAWSOME!

Cats are sexy

There's a reason why Catwoman is indisputably the hottest female character in the entire comic-book universe.
Just sayin'.
PAWSOME!

Cats enhance your decor

Years of watching HGTV may have given you the impression that creating a home environment that's simultaneously comfortable and elegant is the kind of thing best left to professionals and those who can afford to hire them.

Stuff and nonsense! Nothing could be further from the truth.

Nobody has more panache, more casual elegance, more of what the French call *je ne sais quoi* oozing from every pore and strand in their body, than the typical housecat. And as far as comfort goes—*beesh,* please! Has anybody ever been more successful at maintaining a near-constant air of comfort and ease than our feline friends?

Here's a thought experiment that will prove just how right I am: Picture your living room as you currently have it decorated. Now picture that exact same room—with all the same furnishings—but, this time, imagine two or three chic moggies lounging about the place.

Looks one hundred percent better already, doesn't it?

So the next time you feel like giving the homestead a bit of a spruce, there's no need to clip pictures from *Better Homes and Gardens* or go into hock at the Home Depot. Stop by your local shelter instead.

Happy home, happy cat, happy life.

PAWSOME!

Cats are excellent judges of character

In his book *Celebrating Cats*, Roger A. Caras writes: "Tradition has it that Adolf Hitler hated cats. He probably did; everything else was wrong with him."

While the point about the profound personality flaws of cat haters is well taken, I'd prefer to think that it was the other way around—that it's not so much that truly detestable people don't like cats. Rather, it's the *cats*—sensing all that detestability—who will avoid such a person at all costs.

I have absolutely no way of proving it, and sadly there aren't any scientific studies (that I'm aware of) to confirm it, but it's been my experience that cats are shrewd and insightful appraisers of human nature. My husband who, when I first met him, believed himself to be "not a cat guy," turned out to be easy pickings for my cat Vashti, who had him wrapped around her snow-white paw inside of a month by a) being gorgeous, and b) singling him out for special, affectionate attention.

(*But she's so pretty, and she likes me!* my husband would protest, whenever I chided him for feeding Vashti from the table, or giving her extra treats at night, or engaging in some other obvious act of feline vassalage.)

The point being, there was a dedicated cat lover lurking inside my husband-to-be all along. It simply took the keenly observant eye of a cat to suss it out.

Every cat I've ever met has known within nanoseconds that I'm a complete sucker, utterly unable to resist a pair of sad eyes or a pleading paw placed on my knee before I cave in and do whatever the kitty in question wants. When I was a kid, cats used to follow me on my way to school, and they'd have me dispensing the food from my lunchbox faster than a mobster shakes down the owners of a mom-and-pop grocery store.

And I've never known a single person who my cats thoroughly despised—instantly and upon meeting them—who turned out to be worth a darn.

So the next time you're wondering whether some new acquaintance is all they're cracked up to be, bring them around for your cat to size up. If they turn out to be a less-than-desirable companion, believe me your cat will know—and she'll make sure you do, too.

Nothing beats feline intuition, which is powerful and **PAWSOME!**

Zoomies!

When was the last time you ran around like a maniac for no other reason than the glory of movement itself? The ecstasy of pumping energy back into your muscles after lying down for a long time? To chase an imaginary squirrel or playmate you'd made up in your head? Just for the sheer, irrepressible *joy* of it?

Because your cat does that all the time. And it's

PAWSOME!

(Except for the not-so-pawsome 4:00 a.m. zoomies...what is *up* with that???)

Poop zoomies!

There's no consensus opinion as to why, exactly, some cats will hightail it away from the litter box the second they're done using it as if they were fleeing a crime scene. Bashfulness? Self-consciousness? Some residual evolutionary fear of predators sniffing them out?

For the record, cats in the wild don't flee their poop. Assuming, of course, that you and your vet have ruled out any digestive issues, it seems that the four *actual* potential answers to this question are:

- Because it's hilarious

- Because cats are deeply weird

- Because your cat wants you to be aware—and appropriately admiring—of her latest...um..."accomplishment"

- Because your cat doesn't want to be standing too close to any incriminating evidence when someone in your house says, "Do you smell something *odd*?"

No matter how bad a day I'm having, "poop zoomies" (mostly perpetrated by my cat Fanny, an odd and self-conscious little sprite of a cat) will always crack me up.

And anything that generates a guaranteed laugh is, without question, **PAWSOME**!

Dat ass

I f I had a nickel for every time I've awakened first thing in the morning to find a cat bum wedged firmly against my face, I'd have a mountain of nickels stretching higher than the Matterhorn.

I'm guessing that you, dear reader, can say the same.

Cats love showing off their butts. There's the tail lift, the back-side bump (when your cat, walking past you, casually bonks his hindquarters against your shin), the "elevator butt," (when you're scratching your cat's back near the base of his tail and he raises his hindquarters in response), the full-on face plant (and the aforementioned waking up nose to...er..."nose" with a feline derriere).

For sheer inventiveness in coming up with so very many ways to work their butts into the conversation, as it were, our cats deserve to be commended. *Look at it!* seems to be their constant demand. *Admire it! Behold my butt in all its terrible glory!*

Students of feline psychology will offer all sorts of scientific explanations to account for why cats are so fascinated with making sure *we're* so fascinated with their backsides. And while I'm sure that's all completely legit, let's be honest: Cats are constantly showing off their butts because they think—nay, they *know*—that their butts are worth showing off. And however much we may protest, we feel the same.

We love cat butts. We can't get enough of cat butts. We're practically cat-butt junkies.

Scoff at me all you like, but as Exhibit A I invite you to visit Amazon and do a search for "cat butt coloring books." Go ahead, I'll wait.

By the time you come back here—having made your way past dozens of pedestrian titles like "Cat Butts: A Coloring Book" and "A Cat Butt Birthday" all the way to "Cat Butts in Space: The Feline Frontier"—you'll have to concede the point. And that's before we even delve deeper (ahem) into the virtual Aladdin's Cave of cat butt swag available on the open market for the discerning ailurophile: cat butt stickers, cat butt calendars, cat butt refrigerator magnets, cat butt necklaces and earrings, cat butt wine-bottle stoppers, cat butt tissue holders (because who *wouldn't* want to pull a fresh Kleenex out of a cat's wazoo?), cat-butt-shaped shoulder bags, cat butt t-shirts and hoodies, crocheted cat butt coasters, cat butt coffee mugs...

I could go on (I really could, because all this stuff is still only the tip of the cat butt iceberg), but I feel like my point's probably been made.

My own personal theory as to why we're so oddly enamored of kitty tushes goes something like this: Cats lift their tails to show us their butts when they're particularly happy with us, and in doing so they've trained us to be particularly happy when we're "rewarded" with that upward flick.

Not to mention that there's something indisputably aesthetically pleasing about the perfectly round and puckered pimento nestled back there in our cats' nether regions, and we may as well just admit it. And who among us, upon observing the jaunty little sway of a cat's behind as she walked away, hasn't found themselves thinking, *Shake it, don't break it, baby!*

The bottom line (hee!) is that cat butts are among the consistently greatest butts out there. And if you're a person who lives with a cat, then you're lucky enough to have daily access to one in all its sassy, saucy, seein'-is-believin' splendor.

PAWSOME!

Those peepers!

C ats have some of the most beautiful eyes in the world...

And sometimes their eyes look like lasers!

PAWSOME!

Cats are graceful.
Except when they're not.

T his is a true story:

My lithe little Fanny—a delicate and fine-boned ballerina of a cat—leapt nimbly four feet up from the floor to our six-inch-wide marble mantelpiece and deftly wended her way across it, weaving among the framed photos, vases, and candlesticks without so much as grazing a single one. In one graceful bound, she then flew from the mantelpiece to the even-narrower (perhaps three inches wide) back of the sofa, and stealthily cat-walked her way from one end to the other before gently descending back down to the floor ten feet away from where she'd originally started, noiseless as a cloud in her dismount.

I'm not sure what the point of the expedition was other than, possibly, to impress the two klutzy, graceless humans who were watching her. (That would be my husband and me, and we were suitably impressed.)

The very next day, the same cat tried to leap from the floor onto our coffee table, which is a mere eighteen inches high and wide as the side of a barn. There was one—and only one—thing on that enormous coffee table, other than a few tasteful photography books: a small dish of salsa resting next to a plate of chips. Given how very large the entire landing surface of the table was, and how comparatively small the bowl of salsa, you'd almost have to be aiming right for it to hit it.

Nevertheless, that's exactly what Fanny did. Caught one paw in the bowl, which promptly flipped into the air before coming to rest (spilling its contents, naturally) on a white, faux-fur shag rug. Fanny herself didn't even stick the landing, but rather tumbled tush over teacup onto the ground, landing in a clumsy heap of fur.

Moral of the story: Cats are graceful. Except when they're not.

And that little bit of unpredictability is just one more thing that makes living with cats so very entertaining...

And so very **PAWSOME**!

"Making biscuits"

I don't know about you, but I love a knead-y cat.

Not all cats "make biscuits"—which is when a cat pushes in and out with his paws, alternating between left and right—but lots of them do. As with all things cat-centric, there's no one clear-cut answer as to why cats do this (comfort and scent-marking are two big contenders), although one thing's for sure: If a kitty's kneading on you, it's an unmistakable sign of affection and contentment.

My cat Clayton adores kneading on soft things, like our mushiest pillows. His other favorite thing to "make biscuits" on is the roll of flesh just above the waistband of my jeans. Which I guess means that my belly and our mushiest pillows are (from Clayton's perspective, anyway) of a similar texture and consistency. Which *definitely* means I'll be demanding a refund on my Abs Roller, posthaste.

PAWSOME!

Cats are perfect miniature space heaters

B ack in the Olden-Time Days of Yore (an official term I just made up), before the advent of central heating, figuring out the best way to heat a bed on a cold winter's night was a devilishly tricky conundrum.

In the Middle Ages, a servant might heat a brick or large rock in the fireplace and then rub it on the bedsheets—although warming your sheets with a rock, only to have them get cold again ten minutes later, was probably even less fun than it sounds. Fancy metal bed warmers, which replaced heated bricks, worked roughly the same way (fill them with hot embers, rub them all over the sheets) and, again, produced temporary-at-best results, along with the constant danger of scorching the bed linens. Hot-water bottles eventually came along to replace bed warmers, but they were made of rubber and apt to wear thin eventually or just plain wear out—not to mention that you'd inevitably (and rather unpleasantly) wake up the next morning to find a *cold* rubber bottle of water in bed with you.

Yuck, yuck, and *yuck*.

This is a prime example of humans working awfully hard to solve a problem that nature already solved for us a long time ago. Your trusty feline's normal body temperature runs just a scooch above yours (in the 99.5 to 102.5 degree range) and isn't prone to cooling overnight—like, say, that rubber water bottle is. Plus, cats are just the right size to fit snugly under the covers without taking up more space than is comfortable for the sprawl of your own arms and legs. So having a deliciously warm and furry friend cuddled deep beneath the blankets with you, by your feet or at your side, is an excellent way to stave off the cold when the thermometer plunges.

And if you can work it out so that you have two or three or even *four* cats to pile into bed with you (literally—it's best when they all just pile right on top of you), then you'll be in an enviable position, indeed. I'm talking about a blissful purr-puddle of body heat—albeit one that will make it excruciatingly difficult for you to get out of bed the following day. (Is there anything better than cuddling in bed with your kitties on a frosty winter morning?)

On the other hand, those warm and cozy overnight hours will be deeply sublime.

Confession: Sometimes in the winter, when I'm writing at the desk in my home office—wearing socks but no shoes, naturally enough—I'll move one of the cats' beds so that it's directly below my feet, thus tempting said cat to curl up curl up close enough to my toes (or even directly on top of my toes) to keep them comfy and warm, no matter how bone-chillingly cold it gets outside.

Toasty toes all January long? **PAWSOME!**

Cats can operate NASA spacecraft

I swear it's true.

Well...it's sort of true.

Daniel Lakey is a NASA spacecraft-operations engineer who works on the European Space Agency's Solar Orbiter, an unmanned spacecraft that circles the sun and sends back all kinds of information to scientists here on Earth.

Like just about everybody else with an office job, Lakey was ordered to work from home during the Covid-19 crisis—where, as reported to *The Atlantic*, he was subjected to the not-so-tender mercies and constant interference of his two feline housemates, Sparkle and Buttons.

Sparkle, in particular, was fond of commandeering Lakey's computer keyboard—both while Lakey was at his desk performing the task of managing a solar orbiter millions of miles from Earth, and also whenever he left his computer unattended.

Of course, there are plenty of fail-safes in place to keep a cat from *actually* directing the orbital path of a NASA spacecraft. Still, cats are pretty handy with a keyboard once they've taken one over, as anyone with cats can f02g%$*#23g;jhldf!$#!

Apparently, Sparkle isn't the only NASA-affiliated feline with sky-high as*purr*ations. On April 7th, astrophysicist Amber Straughn tweeted:

Actually discussed in a virtual meeting today: how to keep cats from accidentally commanding spacecraft while this work is going on in people's homes on laptops instead of inside a cat-free NASA building. #catsofquarantine

And there you have it.

So the next time you hear a report of a UFO sighting, consider the possibility that what's been spotted overhead is a spacecraft that very much originated here on planet Earth—but that's temporarily veering wildly off course because it's fallen into the fuzzy clutches of Sparkle or Buttons, or some other furry miscreant whose human servant is a NASA employee.

Godspeed, brave space kitties of the sky! You have the right stuff, and you're absolutely **PAWSOME!**

Cats are pros at social distancing

"Social distancing" is one of those expressions you probably never heard once in your whole life until sometime circa March of 2020—and then, suddenly, you heard it *everywhere*. Constantly. All the freaking time.

In the era of Covid-19, the gist of "social distancing" is this: Stay home for the most part. Avoid crowds of more than a few people. Stand at least six feet away from anybody you don't live with.

In other words, do exactly what your cat has already been doing her entire life *by choice*.

Cats: once again ahead of the curve, leaving the rest of us racing to catch up.

Because cats are brilliant. And they're also **PAWSOME!**

Cats make the best napping buddies

A midafternoon nap—known in Spanish as a *siesta*—is possibly the most civilized custom that the entirety of Western civilization has ever produced.

Sadly, however, *siestas* aren't looked upon in a favorable light outside of Spain and Latin America. While a midday nap can make it possible to both get up earlier and stay up later—thus extending your potentially productive daily hours in both directions—and while study after study has shown that the human body tends to crave a brief nap in the 2:00 p.m. range, people who make a habit of napping in the middle of the afternoon are generally regarded as loafers. Idlers. Vagabonds and layabouts.

But napping is awesome, and nobody understands that better than your cat. In fact, nobody in the world understands *anything* better than your cat understands napping. Your cat possesses encyclopedic knowledge and *very* strong opinions on everything from ideal nap durations to best practices for choosing and maintaining a nap position, not to mention a minute understanding of the subtle pros and cons when comparing various napping surfaces (mattress versus floor versus sofa versus windowsill versus easy chair...et cetera).

So if you're looking for a partner in crime who will not only approve of your socially frowned-upon midday nap, but who will probably form the sagacious opinion that, *This may be the smartest thing I've ever seen her do*, look no further than your feline best bud.

I don't know about you, but sometimes—when I walk into the bedroom to find one or both of my cats sprawled out and snoozing across the bed in unselfconscious, luxurious bliss—I think to myself that nobody makes napping look so *good* as my cats do. And on those occasions when I indulge in my own midday *siesta*, I never nap more restfully than I do when my cats pile into bed with me, warmly purring their very strong approval of what is, in their opinion, an infinitely wise life choice that I've made.

I'm not sure why it is, but something about falling asleep with one cat leaning heavily against my leg, and the other curled up in the crook between my arm and my torso, makes me fall asleep more quickly, sleep more deeply, and wake up more refreshed than if I were going it alone. Maybe it's the warm glow of approval and acceptance I drift off to dreamland basking in, or maybe there's some actual physiological explanation to account for this.

Maybe it's both.

All I can tell you is that if you haven't tried it already, you definitely should. Those guilt-free afternoons you spend napping the nap of the just—your furry little *siesta* gurus cuddled up at your side—will be blissful, restful, and one hundred percent **PAWSOME!**

Cats are so soft...

L ike, seriously—*sooooooooooooo* soft.

The only thing softer might be a sable. But good luck getting a sable to come live in your house and purr in your lap.

A cat, however, will do just that—allowing you to sink your fingers deep into that thick, soft, luxurious fur—for very little more than the price of a litter box, some annual vet visits, and a heaping helping of lifelong, unconditional love.

PAWSOME!

KITTENS!

Kittens! Kittens! Kittens! Kittens! Kittens! Kittens! Kittens! Kittens!
Kittens! Kittens! Kittens! Kittens! Kittens! Kittens! Kittens! Kittens!
Kittens! Kittens! Kittens! Kittens! Kittens! Kittens! Kittens! Kittens!
Kittens! Kittens! Kittens! Kittens! Kittens! Kittens! Kittens! Kittens!
Kittens! Kittens! Kittens! Kittens! Kittens! Kittens! Kittens! Kittens!
Kittens! Kittens! Kittens! Kittens! Kittens! Kittens! Kittens! Kittens!
Kittens! Kittens! Kittens! Kittens! Kittens! Kittens! Kittens! Kittens!
Kittens! Kittens! Kittens! Kittens! Kittens! Kittens! Kittens! Kittens!
Kittens! Kittens! Kittens! Kittens! Kittens! Kittens! Kittens! Kittens!
Kittens! Kittens! Kittens! Kittens! Kittens! Kittens! Kittens! Kittens!
Kittens! Kittens! Kittens! Kittens! Kittens! Kittens! Kittens! Kittens!
Kittens! Kittens! Kittens! Kittens! Kittens! Kittens! Kittens! Kittens!
Kittens! Kittens! Kittens! Kittens! Kittens! Kittens! Kittens! Kittens!
Kittens! Kittens! Kittens! Kittens! Kittens! Kittens! Kittens! Kittens!
Kittens! Kittens! Kittens! Kittens! Kittens! Kittens! Kittens! Kittens!
Kittens! Kittens! Kittens! Kittens! Kittens! Kittens! Kittens! Kittens!
PAWSOME!

Cats are natural musicians

They play the cello.

They sing for their supper.

Sometimes they even play the piano!

PAWSOME!

Cats aren't afraid to be alone with their thoughts

Once upon a time, it was taken for granted that there would be certain idle moments in the day—waiting at a stoplight, standing in line at a deli counter—when you would be alone with your thoughts. When there'd be nothing for you to focus on for entire minutes at a time other than your own inner monologue and whatever haphazard ideas might be bobbing along in your stream of consciousness.

But the beeping, buzzing, ubiquitous presence of smartphones seems to have filled up all those "empty" moments in the day and pretty much guaranteed that none of us is ever alone anymore in any truly meaningful sense, much less alone with our thoughts. And while I'm all for maintaining human contact, I sometimes wonder if we've become *afraid* of what we might find rattling around in our heads if we spent a few minutes every day and really looked.

Cats, on the other hand, *adore* being alone with their thoughts and never seem to worry about what they might find germinating in the deep dark recesses of their feline psyches. Looking thoughtfully out of a window or straight ahead into empty space is one of your cat's favorite ways to pass the time, when she isn't sleeping. And while it's impossible to know precisely what's running through a cat's mind at any given moment, who—upon seeing the contemplative expression in those mysterious, Sphinx-like eyes—could doubt that it's something infinitely fascinating and wise?

Okay, so maybe what your cat is *actually* thinking is more along the lines of, *I'd love to murder that bird on the windowsill...* But, still! At least cats aren't freaked out by their own murderous impulses.

The Buddha once said that the path to Enlightenment begins with learning how to think, how to wait, and how to fast. And while I'm one hundred percent confident that no cat will ever master the whole fasting thing, cats' superior skills when it comes to waiting and thinking clearly mean they're farther down that Enlightenment path than we are.

In which case, we can only benefit from having their **PAWSOME** example shining before us!

Cats remind us that being curious and being persistent are two great ways to go through life

S top me if this sounds familiar: While you're generally happy to share just about everything in your life and your home with your cat, there's *one* thing in your house—one shelf, one cabinet, one big box of holiday goodies—that you'd prefer Patches kept her fuzzy little paws away from.

And naturally, cats being the perverse creatures they are, that's the precise shelf, cabinet, and/or box that Patches finds completely irresistible.

I remember a few years back, when a reader sent me a huge carton filled with those miniature felt-covered toy mice for me to distribute at some of the cat shelters where I do readings. My black cat Fanny—a lithe little imp if ever there was one—*adores* those miniature toy mice. Fanny also makes a determined point of sticking her nose into every box, bag, and parcel that finds its way into our house, believing (not entirely without reason) that, in doing so, she's apt to discover things she'd probably enjoy, but that I would be unlikely to share with her. Sensing disaster as soon as I opened one flap of this cardboard box of and saw what was inside, I therefore bundled it way into a back corner of our rarely used guest-room closet.

But, of course, my attempt at keeping it hidden from the keenly observant and fiendishly clever Fanny was doomed from the start. About a week later, I came home to a bonanza of tiny felt-covered toy mice strewn across the guest bedroom, the main bedroom, and the living room.

That was the day when I spent over one hundred dollars to replace a bunch of tiny toy mice, and the day when Fanny got a hundred brand-new toy mice all at one time.

The moral of the story—at least from Fanny's perspective—is that curiosity and persistence pay off.

There's a certain kind of person who's fond of quoting the old adage, *Curiosity killed the cat.* Such people only get away with their party-poopery, however, by conveniently lopping off the second half of that saying, which tells us, *But satisfaction brought him back.*

Being consistently curious is a wonderful way to go through life. Curious people learn more things and know more things. They're better conversationalists, and they're constantly engaged with the world. Curiosity is one of those habits of mind that will keep your mind young long past the point when it's gotten difficult—if not impossible—to keep your body in the same condition.

And as a bona fide bestselling author who's nevertheless racked up more than twenty rejections for every one acceptance I've ever gotten, I can attest from hard-won experience that persistence, in this life, is everything.

Cats are born knowing this already.

So the next time you find yourself sighing with exasperation over a handful of Q-tips (now repurposed as ad hoc cat toys) that your frisky feline discovered on a bathroom shelf during one of his daily reconnaissance missions, remember not to be *too* irritated.

Think of your cat as a live-in life coach, guiding you through the intricacies of making the most of your time on this earth. There are, after all, foolish rich people who pay thousands of dollars to actual human life coaches in exchange for a service that *you* are getting entirely for free, from your very own cat.

PAWSOME!

Cats are easy to entertain

Maybe you think of yourself as the life of the party. Or, maybe you struggle to overcome the sense that you're the dull party guest who the other guests wish they hadn't gotten stuck talking to on their way to the bar.

If you're like most of us, you probably toggle somewhere between those two polarities, landing closer to one end of the spectrum or the other depending on your mood, what kind of hair day you're having, or how many new and interesting anecdotes you've shored up since the last time everyone got together.

This is one among thousands of reasons why spending time with cats is so, *so* great—because cats are just about the easiest audience ever. Smart as they are, it's nevertheless almost ridiculously simple to entertain a cat. A laser pointer will do the job, or a bottle cap, or an errant feather from a pillow wafting in the air. You could attach a bird feeder to one of your windows, and—presto! Instant Cat TV!

Heck, you could even tie a cotton ball to a piece of string, and staple that string to a stick you found in your yard, and your cat would be all like, *OMG THIS IS GENIUS!!!!!!!!!!!!!!!!*

In short, nobody will ever make you feel like a more fascinating and naturally gifted entertainer than your cat will. And to paraphrase another legendary entertainer, the late great Jackie Gleason:

"How **PAWSOME** it is!"

Cats shred toilet paper, tissues, and paper towels

O n the downside, it can be rather vexing to have little Jinxie blithely lay waste to so many paper goods when the price of *everything* is going up and up—and when it's not like she's going to stick around to help you clean up the mess she's just made.

On the upside, though, it kinda looks as if a super-festive ticker-tape parade has just passed through your house.

You can even pretend the parade was thrown for you, just 'cause you're so **PAWSOME**!

Cats knock things off of tables and shelves

Hear me out!

Yes, I *totally* understand how this might actually seem like one of the (very few) *annoying* things about living with cats. Sure, it's hilarious when you're watching a video of *somebody else's* cat knocking glassware or pottery off a kitchen counter. That isn't your problem, after all. You can afford to chuckle at *that* person's expense as you cast a smug look over at your own Shadow or Snowball, adorably curled up on the couch—sleeping so angelically that you can practically see a little halo floating above her head.

It's decidedly less funny, however, when the object that's going down is one that's in your very own house—when the cat in question is *your* cat, and what's being destroyed is one of the set of long-stemmed, hand-blown champagne glasses that you wrapped in a dozen newspapers and carefully packed in five soft t-shirts before carrying them all the way back from your vacation in Stockholm (true story); or the photo of your great-grandparents' wedding, framed in irreplaceable antique glass and bequeathed to you by your grandmother (also a true story); or the unattended glass of water you left on the coffee table for *two seconds*, only to see your cat swipe it down onto the hardwood floor FOR ABSOLUTELY NO REASON—LIKE, SERIOUSLY, *NO REASON AT ALL!*—and *now* you have to spend the next half-hour crawling around on your hands and knees with a flashlight so you can make super-extra-one-hun-dred-percent sure it hasn't left behind any tiny little shards you might have missed, and that will *definitely* find their way into a hapless foot or feline paw if they remain undiscovered. (Like pulling a thousand glass splinters out of your own foot wouldn't *still* be better than having to delve into your cat's paw with a pair of tweezers and a tube of antiseptic ointment...)

Ahem.

I feel your pain, is what I'm saying. But consider this: How many times, over the years, have you unwrapped a wed-ding/housewarming/graduation/hostess gift, only to discover some truly heinous—some genuinely hideous and godawful mon-strous—vase/pitcher/picture frame/what-have-you, that you not only have to demonstrate gratitude for ("I've always wanted a set of drinking glasses with Pamela Anderson's face on them!"), but that you're actually expected to *display* in some prominent place? ("These are going right on the bar cart where everybody can see them!")

Sure, you can discreetly pack them back up and stick them high on some unreachable closet shelf as soon as the gift-giver departs. Don't think for a minute, though, that said gift-giver won't notice the items are missing the next time they come over to your house. ("Hey—what happened to those Pam Anderson glasses I got you?")

If you live with a cat, however, you have an easy and obvious way out. "You know how Tiger is," you'll be able to reply, casting your eyes down with just the right amount of feigned disappointment. "She knocked them clean off the bar cart, and they shattered into little bits." And then, with a despondent sigh, you can add, "She's a stinker, all right, but what can you do?"

Problem solved!

The best part is that your cat—who, let's face it, is ENTIRELY unrepentant even when she destroys something that you actually do love—won't mind at all if you pin the blame on her. She won't lose one single second of sleep, out of the roughly fifty-seven thousand seconds she spends sleeping every day, for worrying about it.

Having a fuzzy little love bug who lives in your house and plies you with purrs? That's amazing.

Having a partner in crime who's willing to take all the blame and provide you with an airtight alibi?

That's **PAWSOME**!

Cats are experts at getting comfortable

A nd they always make snoozing look sooooooo good...

PAWSOME!

Cats heroically sacrifice themselves to protect you from bad news

S ometimes you don't even know the grenade is there until someone else bravely throws themselves on top of it just to save you.

Case in point, the newspaper I intended to open the other morning. Just as I was about to peruse Page One headlines blaring their
end-times updates of plague, pestilence, and economic carnage,
however, my cat Fanny ran at a gallop from clear across the room,
took a nimble flying leap high into the air, and landed smack in the
middle of the newspaper. She then flopped onto her side and flung
out all four of her legs—so as to achieve maximum sprawl—before
rolling adorably onto her back.

She was so very adorable, in fact, that the irresistible,
weapons-grade force of her adorableness reduced me to a simpleton,
babbling helplessly in her direction (*Who's a silly girl? Who's my
silly, silly girl?*), while my gallant Fanny—with no concern for what
effects the day's dreadful news might have on *her*—flopped back
onto her stomach and began happily clawing up the paper beneath
her, effectively shredding it to bits and thus sparing me from an
unbearably depressing morning.

It was a close call.

In households all over the world, every single day, this same ritual
of self-sacrifice is repeated by fearless felines of all description. Cats
both old and young, slim and portly, aloof and clingy, hyperac-
tive and brazenly lazy, are bravely shielding their beloved human

companions—*using their own bodies!*— from any incursion by the horrors contained in innocent-looking daily newspapers.

Most of us, while we're either sighing in frustration over our pilfered paper (*Bad kitty! That's* mommy's *newspaper!*) or affectionately rubbing the ears of the cat perched atop it, will never know just how close a brush with disaster we had.

Everyone loves to talk about the altruism of dogs. But dogs make such a big *show* of guarding their humans—forever barking and growling and jumping, and generally making such a spectacle of themselves—that *of course* you're basically *forced* to commend their protectiveness. (Even when they're "protecting" you from perfectly helpful people, like the mail carrier or the delivery driver with your takeout chicken, which is a mistake your cat will never make.)

True heroes toil in the shadows, where their heroism is generally misunderstood or overlooked altogether. But know, beloved feline companions, that some of us are aware how very deep your sacrifice goes.

And, to us, you will always remain the very embodiment of **PAWSOME!**

Cats like to catch bugs

D o you like catching bugs in *your* house?

I don't like catching bugs in *my* house.

Fortunately for all of us, cats love catching bugs! Nothing makes a cat's day like the opportunity to dismember a cockroach, dispatch a housefly, or tackle the horror-movie-sized spider that's terrorizing you in the bathroom. A task so thoroughly unpleasant as to constitute a mild form of mental torture (to squish, or not to squish? <<shudder>>) is the equivalent of a three-day holiday weekend kicked off by concerts and fireworks, as far as your cat is concerned.

Best of all, your wily feline will almost always get her man...er...bug.

Less expensive than hiring a professional exterminator and way, *way* cuter.

PAWSOME!

Cats go perfectly with books

F ormula for the *purr*fect Sunday:

Sunlight in the windows, birdsong in your ears, a good thick book in your hands, and a warm, purring cat in your lap.

PAWSOME!

Raspy tongues

If you were blindfolded and trying to pick out a cat from among a bunch of other animals, using only your sense of touch, it might not be as easy as you'd think. Soft fur wouldn't be much of a tip-off, for example—just about every mammal, especially the domesticated ones who share our homes with us, have fur. Tails are also pretty ubiquitous. Same goes for claws and sharp teeth. Running your hand over a snout-full of whiskers wouldn't be much of a help; cats have whiskers in common with dogs, ferrets, rats, gerbils, horses, and even seals and walruses.

But there's nothing quite so distinct, so *paw*sitively and unmistakably feline, as a cat's raspy tongue. In fact, to have felt a cat's raspy tongue along your arm even once is to be able to pick out the raspy tongue of any cat anywhere—even while blindfolded.

The reason why feline tongues have their trademark rasp is because they're covered in a type of hooked, hollow bristle called *filiform papillae*. You've probably already heard that these bristles help cats clean and detangle their fur during the grooming process. The barbs on cats' tongues also help them to rasp the meat from the bones of their prey.

That's why raspy tongues are good for our cats. They're good for *us*, however, simply because they're...well...because they're so *raspy*. It might seem contradictory to describe a feeling as being both "rough" and also "affectionate," and yet what two words better apply to the sandpapery sensation of being lovingly "groomed" by your cat?

Being licked by his own mama cat when he was a kitten is the first tactile memory that any cat has. His mom would have licked him clean immediately after he was born, and used her tongue as a combination washcloth and scent marker all over the kitten's coat, ears, and every part of his tiny body when he was still very small. So when your cat includes you now in this deeply ingrained ritual of love, it's hard to imagine a higher compliment.

(Just so long as your cat doesn't "compliment" you for too long. Remember: those barbed tongues were designed to strip the meat off of bones!)

It's very sweet when a dog enthusiastically licks you, but dogs' tongues have a *slight* tendency to be just a *wee* bit spit-riddled and (sorry!) even slimy—two sins that your cat's tongue will almost certainly never commit.

And that, once again, is because cats' tongues are just so, *so* raspy. **PAWSOME!**

Cats will warm your favorite chair for you

I haven't had to sit in a cold chair or climb into a chilly bed since 1995.

That was the year when I first started living with cats.

I've seen my cats devote hours—heck, I've seen them devote entire *days*—to thoughtfully warming up my favorite easy chairs, sofa cushions, and bed pillows for me. Sometimes they'll sacrifice so many of their own leisure hours to ensuring my comfort that I have to *beg* them to stop, to plead with them that it really is okay, that they've warmed up the recliner sufficiently to protect my posterior from any possible contact with a less-than-toasty surface, and that all I want now is to relax and watch whatever new version of *The Great British Bake Off* Netflix is promoting these days.

Still, it can take as long as a full half-hour of imploring (sometimes I have to implore at the top of my lungs) before I'm finally able to persuade my conscientious kitties that they've done enough to help me for one day and can get up now. (*Seriously, guys—get up now!*)

That's how devoted to me my cats are.

It's a kind of dedication to service—a selflessness, really—that on doesn't encounter very often these days.

But when you do, and especially when it's being demonstrated by your very own cats, it's a **PAWSOME** thing to behold!

Cats know how to throw shade

D o you ever think your problem is that you're just too *nice*? Do you sometimes wish you knew how to crush people into insignificance with a single, withering gaze?

Good news: your cat is here to help! When it comes to throwing a single scornful glance—the kind that doesn't necessarily make you feel invisible, but kinda makes you wish you were—nobody can hold a candle to your supercilious and somewhat snobbish feline. With a single disdainful sniff, or one cool glance before turning her head away, your cat, when she wants to, is very eloquently able to convey the message: *Leave me now, worm.*

Your mileage may vary, but suffice it to say that when I've had guests in my home over the years who one or more of my cats didn't care for, nobody was ever in any doubt as to how the cats felt. In particular, my surly girl Scarlett—who never met a stranger she had the smallest particle of use for—had a way of turning her backside, flicking her tail dismissively, and stalking coldly away that might have abashed Queen Elizabeth herself, had the Queen for some reason found herself of an afternoon taking tea in our Midtown Manhattan high-rise.

(Good god, I miss that cat so much!)

My point isn't that cats are actually the mean-spirited creatures naysayers try to make them out to be. But those naysayers tend to be the kind of people who don't like cats—and who cats therefore, in their infinite wisdom, show their colder side to—and that kind of *is* the point.

In short: Don't waste time on the haters. Give them the haughty side-eye and move on with your day.

You'll be glad your **PAWSOME** cat showed you how!

Naming a cat is super fun!

Cats the musical has divided the opinions of theater aficionados since long before its big-screen adaptation became a conspicuous flop. But even the most jaded theatergoer would have to concede that the names of *Cats*' feline characters may be the most entertaining roster in theater history: Bustopher Jones, Jennyanydots, Skimbleshanks, Rum Tum Tugger, Bombalurina, Rumpleteazer, Mister Mistoffelees, and Grindlebone, to name just a few.

We can't all have a gift for wordplay like the great poet T.S. Eliot, author of the delightful *Old Possum's Book of Practical Cats*, upon which *Cats* is based. Still, each time we adopt a cat, we have the opportunity to let our imaginations roam free—to go beyond Socks, Smoky, Mittens, or Midnight and flex our creative muscles.

I, myself, have been the proud kitty custodian of Scarlett (named for her tendency to faint in her early kitten-hood), Vashti (named for the beautiful Persian queen), my blind cat Homer (an homage to the blind Greek poet), Clayton "the Tripod" (named for the one-legged tap dancer Clayton "Peg Leg" Bates), and Fanny (a family name—I had great-aunt Fannys on both sides—although my UK readers are forever reminding me of its less-innocent connotations).

While writing this book, I asked my readers to contribute the names of their own cats, as well as the best and worst cat names they'd ever heard. Here's an entirely unscientific sampling of the results:

The Good:

Bobaloo, Earl Grey, Oliver, Kerfuffle, Blackula, Paw McCatney, Penelope, Momo, Rigatoni, Casper, Herman, Vixen, Thumbelina, Boris and Natasha, Death and Taxes (two black cats), Pickles, Maggie, Tumbleweed, Oscar, John Henry, Jim Morrison, Ziggy, Nico, Sabrina, Max, Hermes, Jojo, Chairman Meow, Gypsy Rose, Bubbles, Peanut, Trixie, Fonzie, Hendrix, Hercules, Lancelot, Houdini, Figaro, Gus, Frida Cat-lo, and Noodles

The Bad:

Dog, Dawg, Bluecifer, Baby Jesus, Darth Kitty, Puss, Natas (Satan spelled backward), Cat, Other Cat, Smelly Cat, Cutie Patootie, Chicken Nugget, Fatness Neverclean (presumably a riff on Katniss Everdeen from the *Hunger Games* books), Fluffy Fusty Feather Fungus, Dot Com, Mocha Latte, Fruity Pebbles, Peepants, Gus 2, Final Gus, and Gus 4: The Re-Gus-ening

The Ugly:

Sh-thead (this was BY FAR the most common response I got when I asked for the worst cat names my readers had ever heard), Penis Face, Hitler, Adolf, Crackhead, Bimbo, Stinky, Stinkus, Mud Butt, Mieskeit (literally Yiddish for "ugly"), Booger, Snot, Scabies, Garbage, Chemo, Mucous, and Spit

Sometimes cats are made of liquid

PAWSOME!

Cats are self-cleaning

Things in your life that you have to clean:

Your floors
Your dishes
Your refrigerator
Your toilet
Your bathtub
Your books, bookcases, CDs, picture frames, and assorted knick-knacks
Your clothes
Your kitchen counters
Your toddler
Your dog

Things in your life that are self-cleaning:

Your cat
Maybe your oven?

When it comes to household chores, your cats are all about simplifying your life.
PAWSOME!

Cats hang out with you in the bathroom and never, ever judge

The great mass of humanity as a whole can't come to a uniform consensus on just about anything, from politics to religion to the very best toppings for pizza. (Pineapple pizza, for the record, is an abomination in the eyes of the Lord.)

But the one thing we can pretty much all agree on is that 99.99% of what we do in the bathroom, we want to do in absolute privacy. No matter what it is that's brought you in there—whether it's related to health, hygiene, grooming, or digestion—chances are you'd recoil like a vampire in sunlight if somebody were to suddenly fling the bathroom door wide open and catch you mid...whatever.

And yet, humans are social animals, and we almost never completely lose our desire for companionship, even when we're engaged in the most private of private acts. That's why so many of us keep our bathrooms stocked with books or transistor radios, or even bring smartphones in, so that even during these most isolated of moments, we can nevertheless remain connected with the outside world.

Not that any of these are a true or adequate substitute for the living, breathing real thing.

Enter the not-so-humble housecat.

I hear from cat-moms and cat-dads all the time who are thoroughly mystified as to *why*, exactly, little Coco or Smokey will insist on following them into the bathroom, and *I'm* always thoroughly mystified by their mystification. Because the truth is that your cat doesn't give a flying fig *what* you're doing in there, so long as she gets to be with you—her very favorite being in the entire universe—while you do it.

It's easy (and painful) to imagine a scenario wherein somebody walks into the bathroom, catches you in the middle of some less-than-attractive act and, as a result, never looks at you quite the same way again.

But there isn't a single thing you could do in the bathroom, or in any room, that would be so odd, off-putting, or downright repulsive that it would make your cat love you one iota less, or judge you to be one less particle awesome than she already thinks you are. She just wants to hang, is all. She's happier being with you than without you, no matter how many raw veggies may currently be working their way through your system. And, that being the case, she simply doesn't understand why you feel the occasional need to disrupt your closer-than-closeness with a resolutely shut bathroom door.

Nobody, in other words, will ever make you feel more known—or less judged—than your cat will. Your cat really and truly *sees* you, all the way down to your literal bottom, and loves you just the same, regardless. She understands that while love may not always be pretty, loving someone only at their most attractive isn't really love at all.

So break out the nose-hair trimmer, uncap the Preparation H, unspool the toilet paper (if your cat hasn't already thoughtfully provided this service), and leave the bathroom door open for kitty to join you if she feels like it. And know, as you do so, that you're the insanely fortunate object of a love that's bona fide, limitless, and one-hundred-percent unconditional in the truest sense of the word.

And that's as **PAWSOME** as it gets!

You're the only one who truly understands your cat

Cats have a reputation for weirdness that's probably not *entirely* deserved. Still, even the most die-hard cat lover would have to admit that cats, at times, can be just the teensiest bit odd.

While many of those little oddities become more explicable the more you understand cats generally, each individual cat has his or her own little *purr*sonality quirks that nobody could ever hope to understand—nobody, that is, other than *you*, the person who knows your cat best.

Only you will know that Mr. Whiskers is unhappy unless permitted to paw open the bottom bathroom sink cabinet and then curl inside it for a nap, or that you're not allowed to refill an ice-cube tray without taking a few of the frozen cubes out for Binx to play "hockey" with, or that Cali waits to walk *down* the stairs until you start walking *up* the stairs so she can pass you at the precise halfway point, or that Tucker insists on licking dry-cleaner's bags, or that Fiona will curl up on a pile of potholders on your kitchen counter to take a nap, but will emphatically *not* be happy if those potholders are replaced with dish towels...

And so on. You get the point.

Over the years, I've stopped asking *why???*when it comes to these small idiosyncrasies that comprise my cats' personalities—rather, I cherish my status as the sole person who can understand them all, and who can make them explicable to other people. (*Clayton won't* *take one of those treats unless you place it in the precise center of an empty dish,* I always have to remind my husband.)

It's just one more hallmark of the uniquely close and **PAWSOME** relationship that you—and you alone—have with your cat.

Cats will never mock your taste in music

C onfession: My guilty-pleasure playlist is embarrassing twice over—both for the specific songs on it, and also for just how much information about my age (ahem) it reveals. Its highlights (or lowlights) include "I Can't Hold Back" by Survivor, "Fight Fire With Fire" by Kansas, "Good Vibrations" by Marky Mark and the Funky Bunch, "Wannabe" by the Spice Girls, and various tracks by Milli Vanilli. (Yes! I liked Milli Vanilli in college! Sue me!)

There's almost nobody around whom I'd feel comfortable blasting "Strut" by Sheena Easton while dancing around my living room—nobody, that is, except my cats, who don't judge me at all for what I listen to in the privacy of my own home, and who never ever ever try to lecture me on the superior merits of Brian Eno or King Crimson. So long as the *Xanadu* soundtrack isn't blaring loud enough to wake the neighbors, my cats are entirely copacetic.

(They also never do that "howl-along" thing that dogs sometimes do—like my childhood dog Brandi did to Richard Marx songs—which always strikes me as kind of judgey.)

Fun fact: "MMMBop" by Hanson was all over the radio the summer I adopted my blind cat Homer, and it still brings back **PAWSOME** memories whenever I hear it!

Cats love how you look,
even on bad hair days

S ome people live hand to mouth. I, apparently, live haircut to haircut. I never fully appreciated just how thin a line separated me from disaster until the state of New Jersey went into lockdown in March 2020 and took my March 21st salon appointment with it.

I have a lot of hair. A *lot* of hair. Hair that's very thick, and very curly, and that grows as rapidly as if my head were a Play-Doh Fuzzy Pumper.

For the first three weeks following my (desperately needed!) missed haircut, things weren't so bad. I was in a kind of '80s-hair-band zone of almost-passable—especially if you were into the whole nostalgia thing. By ten weeks, my bangs had grown so long over my eyes that I could no longer see well enough to drive a car. (Not that it really mattered, since there was no nothing to drive to, anyway.)

By the time quarantine hit the six-month mark, I was Cousin Itt.

Eventually I got vaccinated and could rejoin the outside world, at which point even my entirely non-judgmental husband was looking forward to my first post-lockdown haircut. But I can think of two fuzzy little somebodies to whom the chaotic state of my hair for so many months never made one lick of difference.

That's because cats—much more than even the most adoring person in your life—really and truly don't care *at all* what you look like. How you look never had a single thing to do with how your cat felt about you in the first place, or the very, *very* positive impression they formed of you way back in the beginning of your relationship. So there's absolutely no reason for their opinions to be shaped *now* by something as entirely inconsequential as the ever-changing state of your hair—not even on a hair day so *very* bad that looking in the mirror makes you want to crawl right back into bed.

Not that your cat will ever think getting back into bed is a bad idea.

PAWSOME!

Loving a cat means always having to say you're sorry

I 've never bought the oft-vaunted idea that love means never having to say you're sorry. On the contrary, I've always believed that true love means knowing when you owe the one you love an apology, and then offering that apology sincerely and without hesitation.

Nevertheless, it can be hard to swallow your pride and humbly admit you were wrong. If you're fortunate enough to live with a cat, however, you'll have lots of opportunities to practice—because cats always know *exactly* what you've done wrong.

Here's a handy list of things I've done to irritate my own cats over the years—and that you, more likely than not, have done to irritate yours—to give you a head start. Simply fill in the blank with the appropriate answer or answers. You'll be apologizing like a pro in no time!

"I'm sorry, Muffin, for [blank]"

Waking you up
Breathing too loudly
Sneezing too loudly
Taking your spot on the couch
Sleeping on your side of the bed
Shifting positions while you were napping on top of me
Closing the bathroom door while you were still outside

Closing the bathroom door while you were still inside
Closing any door, at any time, for any reason
Paying attention to the computer/smartphone/television screen instead of you
Touching your toes
Kissing your nose
Rubbing your belly
Petting you with wet hands
Cuddling with Patches longer than I cuddled with you
Singing the Mentos jingle without realizing I was doing it
Meowing back at you
Feeding you too early, too late, and/or with an unacceptable new brand of food
Picking you up
Putting you down
Looking at you funny
Letting the neighbor cat look at you funny
Letting the birds outside look at you funny
Allowing noisy children to ride their bicycles on the sidewalk in front of our house
Anything else not on this list that I may have forgotten
All of the above

Cats: Patiently helping us iron out our kinks, flaws, and very human failings for going on ten millennia now.
   PAWSOME!

Cats wash their privates in public because they straight-up don't give AF

The typical American is never going to be as comfortable on a topless beach as the average French person. And as for being okay with public nudity (or a level of clothes-less-ness that's practically nudity), Brazilians, particularly during *carnivale,* have us all beat.

But when it comes to fully splaying and displaying all the hidden nooks and crannies of one's own body, absolutely nobody can hold even the tiniest candle to your cat. Your cat who will wait until you have ten people over for a dinner party, climb right into the middle of the dining-room table where every single one of your guests can't help but watch her, casually hoist one hind leg high in the air—offering the kind of "panoramic" view of all the goodies that, among humans, is usually reserved for the doctor's office or waxing salon—and *go to town* for long, *long* minutes with the scouring power of her own pink tongue.

No shame. No inhibitions. Absolutely no rats' asses given.

Like a *boss.*

Because that's what **PAWSOME** looks like.

Cats force you to keep doors open

I once saw a cartoon of a cat standing before the pearly gates of Heaven, with an obviously irritated St. Peter holding them open and admonishing the cat, "Make up your mind! Are you going in or not?"

Below was a caption that read: *How cats end up with nine lives.*

Cats never seem able to make up their minds if they want to be inside or outside. Even indoor-only cats like mine will cry and cry at a closed bedroom door and then, once you've opened the door to let them pass and closed it again behind them, will immediately begin caterwauling anew—only this time from the other side.

But I think that looking at it from such a binary, A/B perspective sort of misses the point. Your cat wants to be both in *and* out—which may sound contradictory, but really just means your cat wants their options to be as open as that door you're so determined to close.

While we do all inevitably have to make choices in life, closing ourselves off from options too quickly—along with new people, new ideas, and new ways of looking at the world—often means we end up jumping at the first thing that comes along, which is a sucker bet your cat would *never* take.

Or, to put it another way, life is often better with open doors.

Also, I suspect that cats secretly find it amusing to watch us jump up and down every thirty seconds, growing more and more exasperated, while they try to make up their minds on the whole in/out question.

It just goes to prove what we've always secretly suspected: Cats have a sense of humor.

PAWSOME!

Cats' purrs prevent heart attacks and help heal bones, muscles, and tendons

S ome people say that laughter is the best medicine. My mom is apt to scoff and insist that, in fact, *medicine* is the best...well, you know. But my mom has a certain tendency toward literal-mindedness, which doesn't stop her from being lots of fun at parties.

Whichever side of the question you come down on, cats have got you covered. Not only do they keep us in figurative stitches as talented natural comedians, but they also help keep us *out* of *literal* stitches, because cats' purrs have the actual, honest-to-gosh ability to make us healthier and help us heal from injuries faster.

There's even science to prove it.

Cats' purrs tend to vibrate at a frequency of between 20 to 150 Hertz (Hz), a range that's been associated with all sorts of health benefits. Vibrations in that range, according to *Scientific American,* can facilitate bone density and the healing of injured bones, muscles, and tendons. According to a 2018 article in *Orthopedics This Week*, research on frequencies that promote bone growth, fracture healing, pain relief, and relief of inflammation show that frequencies between 20 Hz and 150 Hz are healing frequencies. Vibrations in this range can also help decrease the effects of dyspnea (difficulty breathing) in both humans and other cats.

Not convinced yet that cats have magical healing powers? Then consider this: A 2016 study by the University of Minnesota found that cat owners are 40% less likely to suffer heart attacks or cardiovascular disease as compared to owners of other types of pets or non pet owners, and a Canadian study from 2015 published in *Psychology Today* states that living with a cat can lower cholesterol as effectively as medication. A three-year study at the Baker Medical Research Institute in Melbourne, Australia has shown that living with a cat can lower triglycerides, and a State University of New York at Buffalo study found that cat lovers are likelier to have lower blood pressure, reduced heart rate, and less anxiety as opposed to those poor, spiritually impoverished souls living a cat-free existence.

It goes without saying that you should always consult your own doctor before pursuing any course of, or alternative to, medical treatment. Nevertheless, the fact remains that cat lovers don't just live *better* (of course we do—we live with cats!), we also live *longer*.

Who could ask for anything more?

PAWSOME!

Cats' teeny-tiny noses are the height of aesthetic perfection

Especially when they're freckly...

Sometimes they're even shaped like little hearts!

PAWSOME!

Cats love to get high

Normally, "loves to get high" wouldn't exactly be an attractive quality in a living companion. And far be it for me to advocate—or even appear to advocate—for the recreational use of narcotics. Cats may be people too, but people most definitely aren't cats—and what's harmless and endearing in a cat can be anywhere from completely annoying (I say this as the unfortunate alumnus of several college-era relationships with stoner boyfriends) to downright deadly if replicated in humans.

Having gotten that caveat out of the way, however, I'm asking that you please not harsh my mellow—because there's very little in this life as utterly and insanely adorable as the sight of one's normally graceful, self-possessed kitty rolling and flipping with wild-eyed abandon while under the influence of that wacky feline weed *nepeta cataria*, otherwise known as catnip.

If getting my cats get high on catnip is wrong, then I don't wanna be right.

Catnip is a perennial herb that's a member of the mint family—albeit one that produces very different effects from what one normally sees with mint. (No matter how much mint chocolate chip ice cream I consume, it rarely makes me fall to the ground and roll around in pure, unrestrained delight.) The chemical compound that attracts and affects cats is called nepetalactone—which is found in the leaves and stems—although it should be noted that not all cats are responsive to 'nip, and almost no cats younger than six months old are.

But, having lived with five cats who *lost their flipping minds* whenever a pile of catnip or a catnip toy was put in front of them (they were particularly turned on by Maui Meow loose catnip and the *Yeowww!* line of catnip toys), I can tell you that watching a cat get silly on the 'nip is one of the great, great joys of kitty custodianship.

Nepetalactone is a stimulant when sniffed by cats, producing a "high" that's been described in studies as similar to either marijuana or LSD (which scientists figured out...how, exactly?). It's perfectly safe for cats, although eating an excessive amount can lead to stomach upset. And catnip may even have some beneficial effects for humans. When brewed into a tea it has a mildly calming effect similar to chamomile; it's also known to make an effective and nontoxic mosquito repellant.

Not that any of this would justify bogarting your cat's stash. A tea that smooths out your jangled nerves is all well and good, but the entertainment value of watching your beloved kitty companion tumble across the floor in pure catnip abandon?

That's **PAWSOME!**

Head bonks

Like many of you, I have one cat (this would be Clayton, my "tripod") who's our home's self-appointed official greeter. He's the one waiting smack in the middle of the doorway when my husband and I walk in, who immediately introduces himself to any and all newcomers, who gallops over to give returning visitors an enthusiastic "howdedoo!" and warm their laps the moment they've sat down.

Clayton is also our household's dispenser of head bonks—more properly referred to as "head bunting"—which makes a lot of sense, because head bonking is deeply social behavior. So much of what our kitties do to demonstrate their fondness for us seems to come down to the communal sharing of scents, and the same is true with head bonks. When your cat butts you with his head, he's basically attempting to transfer scent from his own forehead scent glands (located in those sparse patches of fur between eye and ear) onto you—not so much to "mark" you, per se, as to make sure the two of you smell alike. You *are* a family, after all.

In the wild, it's the most confident and social cat in the community who goes around head-bonking all the other cats, to make sure everyone has the same scent. Which is why it makes so much sense that Clayton greets and bonks all newcomers within minutes of entry—Clayton's apparent mission in life being to singlehandedly dispel all those rumors about feline "aloofness" and corral as many people as he can into his ever-expanding feline/human herd.

But even without all the scientific explain-y stuff, you already knew intuitively that, when your cat bonks you with his head, that's his way of saying, "I love you."

PAWSOME

Out of all the humans in the world, your cat chose you

While cats will sometimes condescend to live under less-than-ideal circumstances (*somebody* with opposable thumbs has to open those tuna cans, after all), cats—unlike dogs—feel no particular need to bestow their affections on any unworthy object.

Moreover, cats are keen observers of human nature—they can "read" our body language, the tone of our voice, and even our smell and the dilation of our pupils for information about what kind of mood we're in and the thoughts that are running through our brain.

So a cat that loves you (and you'll certainly be able to tell if one does!) doesn't love you because she *needs* to, but because she *chooses* to.

And, given how *purr*ceptive your finicky feline is, if she's chosen *you* out of all the humans on earth as a worthy object for her affections, chances are that you are a pretty exceptional human!

PAWSOME!

Cats are amazing at receiving affection

This one might almost feel like I'm damning cats with faint praise. After all 'tis easier to receive than to give, right?

Most of us, though, actually find it much *harder* to take than to give. We tend to be afraid of seeming like we need too much. Which is silly, since we don't love our cats *less* because of how much attention and affection they're willing to accept from us. We love them more for it! Nobody, upon feeling a blissed-out cat lean harder into their hand and purr in delight, thinks, *This is certainly a bummer.*

Cats remind us that it's okay to accept kind gestures without immediately worrying about how to reciprocate—or to demand immediate reciprocation for our own kind gestures. No one sits there with a ledger book, after all, and counts up all the times they've petted or fed their cat versus the number of great things our cats have done for *us.*

Our cats do the greatest thing of all just by letting us love them. And they know intuitively that, when it comes to the ones we love who truly love us in return, it all comes out even in the end.

In the meantime, it's totally acceptable—and even kinda **PAW-SOME**—to ask the ones we love for a little extra care when we need it.

Cats keep cat haters out of your life

I think there's something genuinely wrong with people who hate cats.

Naturally I realize there are people who, simply as a matter of taste, don't really care for cats. That's not what I'm talking about. I mean the people who flat-out *loathe* cats and take some sort of weird pride in talking *ad nauseam* about their particular affliction. Like the guy who cornered me at a cocktail party once, six months before my memoir about my blind cat was published, and spent a full ten minutes going on and on and *on* about how much he and his wife hated cats.

Look, I may not *love* goats. I don't especially want to hang out with goats. But I understand why goats *exist* and why some people have them. I don't feel like I have to launch into a whole "Goats Are The Worst" diatribe any time somebody offers me a goat cheese salad, just because one time, when I was six, a goat once tried to eat all the hair off my head during a petting-zoo field trip.

Cat haters have a screw loose, is what I'm saying. Scratch the surface of the typical cat hater and you're almost certain to find any number of other deal-breaking character deficiencies: stinginess, pettiness, bad manners, and lord knows what else.

Unfortunately, much like serial killers, cat haters tend to look and talk and act just like you and me. You may not even realize you're deep into conversation with such a profoundly maladjusted person, or working side by side with one, or even (heaven forfend!) about to accept a second date with one, until it's way too late.

This is where your cat has got you covered. If the mere mention of Puss in conversation causes someone's nose to wrinkle with distaste, then you know what you're dealing with. If such a person somehow manages to make it across the threshold of your home unsuspected, the expression of alarm and aversion upon seeing your cat tree will tell you all you need to know about not issuing a *second* invitation.

Not that they'd be likely to accept that invitation, anyway. When it comes to keeping cat haters and other reprobates well beyond your property line, there will never be a better home-security system than your cat.

Heck, a true and unrepentant cat hater might even start avoiding you in *public* places—just to make one hundred percent sure they never again run the risk of running into, or hearing about, your cat. Which is probably the ideal outcome, anyway. I mean, what use do you even have for a joyless, soulless, mental defective like that?

Your cat has just done you the biggest favor ever by giving them the old Puss-in-boot straight out the front door and out of your life, never to be seen or heard from again.

Pretty **PAWSOME**, no?

Cats love drama

I t often surprises me that there aren't more feline stars of the stage and screen, because probably nobody you know has more of an innate sense of drama than your cat.

In fairness, though, I'd hate to be the director trying to give a cat acting notes. (*Ginger, darling, I'm wondering if you could give me juuuuust a hint of disdain...narrow your eyes in disgust for me...a little more...just a bit more...yes! Just the way you're looking at me right now! That's PERFECT!*)

And yet it hardly seems to matter that fewer cats see their names in lights than ought to—because when you're a cat, all the world's a stage anyway.

Shut a cat out of the bedroom or bathroom and she'll either howl at the door in anguish (*WHYYYYYYYYYYYYYYYYY?!!?!?*) or else mew so sadly and plaintively that it sounds as if her very soul is being ripped from her body. Try rubbing your kitty's tempting tummy when she's not in the mood for belly rubs, and she won't just bat your hand away—she'll wrap her entire body around it (teeth included!) as if she were fighting off a life-threatening attack. And if you've ever seen a cat locked in a life-and-death battle with an inanimate toy mouse—flinging it about the room so he can "chase" it down—then you know exactly what I'm talking about.

A cat about to accidentally tumble off a couch will dig her claws in and cling to the cushion as if it were the precipice of a yawning abyss threatening to swallow her up forever. Put food down in front of a cat that he doesn't like, and he'll either take one sniff and recoil forcefully—as if you'd just placed a dish of rotten eggs in front of him—or else begin making frantic digging/burying motions around it, as if to say, *Cover this up! IT'S HIDEOUS!!!*

The *truly* dramatic cat will do both.

There's no doubt about it—the typical cat is the star of her very own reality show that exists only in her head. It can sometimes be exhausting just trying to keep up.

On the other hand, what would we ever do without all the **PAW-SOME** entertainment?

Cats have inspired great artists for centuries

E gyptians were painting cats on the walls of temples and tombs
five thousand years ago, and Chinese artists were painting cats
well before that.

It's not hard to understand why those with a heightened aesthetic
sensibility would find ins*purr*ation in *felis catus*—effortlessly elegant, compact and graceful (usually), cats are the visual equivalent
of poetry.

Here, then, is a brief and by no means complete sampling of
some of world's most famous artists who've also been unashamed
ailurophiles:

Leonardo da Vinci, Henri Matisse, Frida Kahlo, Pablo Picasso,
Salvador Dali, Andy Warhol, Ai Weiwei, Maya Lin, Jean-Michel
Basquiat, Gustav Klimt, Paul Klee, Edward Gorey, Pierre Bonnard,
Marcel Duchamp, Balthus, Hedda Sterne, Frank Stella, Jay DeFeo,
Beatrice Wood, Emily Barto, and Georgia O'Keefe.

Great minds think alike—and some of the greatest artistic minds
ever were convinced that cats are utterly, thoroughly, inspirationally
PAWSOME!

Cats have the fluffiest, mushiest bellies ever

However fluffy your cat may be on her back and along her sides, her belly is guaranteed to be *twice* as fluffy—and fuzzy, and just so incredibly yummy and soft.

Which makes it soooooooooooooooooo vexing that most cats will spring at your hand like a bear trap if you so much as *try* to rub those tempting tummies!

Still, that moment when your cat rolls over on her back and exposes her belly in all its fleecy, feathery, furry glory?

Totally **PAWSOME**!

Sometimes cats sit like couch potatoes

Who can blame them for trying to get comfy when they work so hard all day being **PAWSOME** for us???

Cats will help you make the bed

There are people who find actual joy, and a certain amount of Zen calm, in doing housework. I freely admit that I am not one of them. Watching one of those "let's clean the house!" montages in some family movie—the kind where everybody from mom and dad down to the littlest rug-rat grabs a broom or bucket and cheerfully pitches in, while the power-guitar chords of _This Is Family Fun!_ strum insistently in the background—I'll turn to my husband and say, "So…I guess this is a movie about a bunch of people who all got lobotomized at the same time?"

But there's one household chore that I actually look forward to every week, and that's when it comes time to change the sheets.

Nobody has ever told my cats that housework is kind of a bummer, or that changing sheets even qualifies as housework, so they experience every part of the process with undiluted joy. As soon as I pull the new sheets from the linen closet, they know what's up—racing ahead of me into the bedroom where they stare at the bed with pupils dilated to murderous proportions. _We're going to kill those sheets so hard!_ I yank off the blankets and begin to pull at the old sheets as my cats leap right into the middle of the mattress and cling ferociously, holding on with all their claws as I drag both sheets and cats off the bed. _Wheeeeeeeee!_ I can almost hear them thinking as they soar briefly into the air—two little genies on a magic carpet ride—before landing on the ground. _This is FUN!_

The fun doesn't stop there! How would I even be able to ensure that the new, clean sheets I put onto the bed were straight and airtight without my helpful kitties racing from one corner of the mattress to the other to double-check my work? Sure, it takes twice as long as necessary to accomplish this task—what with my cats burrowing under the fitted sheet as I attempt to smooth it out, or forming their bodies into tight lumps beneath the top sheet and blanket, or bunching up the blanket into a big enough clump that they can lie on their sides and kick at it with their back legs "bunny feet" style, until finally I cry, "Come *on*, you guys!"

If cats could high-five, my cats would definitely be high-fiving on their way out of the bedroom. *We showed those sheets who's boss!*

It's the most mundane of mundane tasks, but the wide-eyed delight with which my cats greet this weekly chore lends an undeniably festive air to the proceedings.

As if it were an unexpected day off from school, or a trip to an amusement park.

PAWSOME!

Cats have selflessly provided us with millions of hours of free online entertainment

There are literally millions of cats on the internet. They caper endearingly for our amusement on YouTube, Tik Tok, Instagram, and Facebook. They're featured players in memes, gifs, and online greeting cards. There are tens of thousands of websites devoted to cat pictures, cat health, cat products, et cetera.

And yet, there aren't actually any cats *on* the Internet, if you see what I mean. They don't log in themselves to any of the many social media accounts opened in their names. They don't browse the web or swipe through apps or chuckle at the umpteenth photo of a cat wearing a silly costume or whose face is, inexplicably, surrounded by a piece of bread. (Why was that a thing, again?)

Which means that everything cats do to entertain us online, they do solely for our benefit. All the many, many hours cats devote to posing, scampering, donning funny hats, falling off of tables, hiding under blankets, knocking things off of counters, meowing in tune to "Twinkle, Twinkle, Little Star," swimming in the ocean, riding skateboards, fighting with dogs over sofa cushions, trying to squeeze into too-small cardboard boxes, walking on their hind legs, soothing fussy babies to sleep, playing the piano—*et cetera*—they do purely out of the goodness of their hearts. Just to make us happy.

Who else gives so much and asks so little in return?

Nobody, that's who.

One more reason why cats are as **PAWSOME** as it gets!

Cats don't make you feel bad when you leave, but they're psyched when you get home

B ack when I was a teenaged babysitter, I remember having temporary charge of many a tiny tot who would wail and sob disconsolately when their parents headed out for the evening. And my own childhood dog Casey—who was particularly attached to me, and who remains the single greatest dog I've ever lived with—would, according to my mom, howl at the front door to our house for a good twenty minutes whenever I disappeared through it.

Not every child or dog reacts quite so dramatically, of course, to routine leave-takings. Still, it's enough to make you appreciate the relative casualness with which our cats greet our departures to work or the store or out for drinks with friends. "See you later, Mittens!" you might call over your shoulder on your way out, only to be rewarded for this small courtesy with a) a blank stare; b) the slight flickering of one eyelid from a cat who's far too deep into a catnap to care even a little about *your* comings and goings; or c) literally nothing at all, because your cat isn't even anywhere in the vicinity of the door to see you off. Why should he be? It's not as if your departure will adversely affect his sleeping schedule—which, if we're being honest, is most housecats' top-of-mind concern at least eighty percent of the time.

And yet, the sleepy-eyed indifference with which your cats see you off couldn't be further from the glad giddiness they greet you with upon your return—the joyful bounding to the door, the leaping and cavorting when you walk through it. They'll race down the stairs or up from the basement or out from under the bed just so they can be correctly positioned to greet you with a lusty *MEOW!* and an ecstasy of head-bonks against your leg the very moment you cross the threshold.

Perhaps it's true that absence makes the heart grow fonder. Maybe while you were gone, your cat had time to wonder, *What if she* never *comes back? WHO WILL FEED ME???* Or perhaps, even though it's a ritual that's repeated day in and day out, the fact that you've returned strikes your cat as being miraculous all anew—just like we humans have those moments when, as we look at the sleeping cat curled up in our lap, it seems far too good to be true that Fate saw fit to bring us together.

In any case, living with a cat means nobody will ever try to lay a guilt trip on you when you head out into the great world beyond your front door. But a furry little someone will always be very, *very* happy to greet you when you return, worn and weary, to the warmth of your own home.

PAWSOME!

The cute and careful way cats lap ice cream from a spoon

If you've ever given your dog table scraps, then you know it is, to a certain extent, a risky endeavor.

For one thing, dogs can be inept at distinguishing fingers from the food dangling at the ends of those fingers—meaning you have to exercise a fair amount of caution, even when indulging a relatively small dog.

Don't get me wrong—I'm a dog lover from way back. Nevertheless, it provides a striking counterpoint for the very thoughtful, very deliberate manner in which your cat approaches something like ice cream being offered on a spoon.

After a judicious period of preliminary sniffing and head tilting (trying, no doubt, to determine the best angle of approach), his little pink tongue will dab at the ice cream very delicately and carefully, with much apparent seriousness devoted to the whole endeavor. My own cats look downright professorial when offered ice cream on a spoon, as if somewhere in their minds they're covering a blackboard with a complex series of equations—*Good Will Hunting* style—while they mentally hammer out the optimal methodology for transferring the frosty treat from spoon to belly. *Perhaps if I turn my head perpendicular to the spoon...*

This thoughtful circumspection, however, will in no way guarantee that a tiny dot of ice cream doesn't end up on your kitty's nose.

And that, my feline-loving friend, is the most **PAWSOME** part!

Cats are natural comedians

C ats are hilarious. It's a fact so indisputable that even people who don't care for cats (but who are nevertheless aware that the internet exists, and that 50% of it is comprised of funny cat videos) would have a hard time denying it—which should make the writing of this particular entry a breeze.

But it's nowhere near as easy as it should be. Partly that's because nothing saps the funny right out of something like trying to explain *why* it's funny. Complicating things further is that there are so many different, and frequently contradictory, theories about cats' innate humorousness. Some say cats are funny because they act so pompous and dignified, while others say it's because cats are so goofy. Some say it's because cats are cute and others say it's because cats *aren't* cute (cats are very serious creatures, doncha know).

Perhaps it's the mystery itself that makes them so amusing.

The one hypothesis that seems closest to the mark is that cats are always *getting into* something. Getting into things on a regular basis, all by itself, will create tons of opportunities for wackiness and hilarity. After all, there aren't any sitcoms whose weekly plots revolve around characters sitting quietly on their living room couch, doing exactly what they're supposed to be doing. Getting into trouble is every cat's specialty and birthright.

So when cats accidentally close themselves into cardboard boxes, root around—tush up—in your bottom dresser drawer, climb to the top of the refrigerator to take a nap and promptly roll right off it, walk on tiptoe around the toilet bowl until they accidentally fall in, or redistribute freshly cleaned socks from the laundry basket to various hidden corners throughout the house, they're simply fulfilling their manifest destiny.

Ultimately, though, maybe it's best to adopt a philosophy of *why ask why?* Cats are hilarious because they *are*. And they've consented to live among us humans—bumbling and foolish though we may be—to keep us laughing through good times and bad.

PAWSOME!

Cats make being lazy look soooooo good...

Doing stuff is overrated.

I realize that's an unpopular point of view in these over-caffeinated, over-stimulated, over-scheduled times. Nevertheless, I remain firm in my opinion that sunny days do *not* have to be spent outdoors, early birds do *not* get all the worms worth having, and devoting entire hours to letting your mind wander will not only add years onto your life—it's also just an inherently good and worthwhile thing to do.

Nobody knows the value of doing nothing at all better than your cat. I talk a lot in this book about the sheer volume of hours cats will spend napping. But if you look at the hours that your cat spends fully awake, it's not like they're especially "productive" or jam-packed with activity. He'll spend at least half of that awake time watching the world outside your windows, or observing you while you perform some cheerless human task like answering emails or mopping the kitchen—or else he's staring off into the middle distance at nothing in particular, thinking about nobody knows what.

The reason why your cat can get away with a level of loafing that, let's face it, you and I could never pull off without being called lazy is because your cat does it with so much *style* as to be above reproach. Cats are natural aristocrats, with their physical grace and ever-so-slightly-aloof 'tudes. Their effortless elegance can't help but make you a bit reticent to call them out for being lazy, or question why they're doing—or *not* doing—something at any given moment. (*Who are you to question me?!*)

And even the cats like my Clayton, who are, perhaps, more aptly described as "doofy" than "deep," are still so very endearing that what else would you even *want* them to do other than sit there being their lovable selves?

The point is that if you want to work a certain amount of laziness into your day-to-day lifestyle (and I really think you should), you'll never find a better Zen-master to not only show you how to do it, but how to *get away with it*, than your very own cat.

Study laziness diligently enough at the paws of your feline guru, and people won't think you're a shiftless loafer when you lounge about—catlike and elegant—doing nothing in particular.

They'll just think you're **PAWSOME**!

Cats make excellent negotiating partners

Negotiations can often be a tense and drawn-out affair. The Hawaiian people have a solution for extreme stalemates called *ho'oponopono*. Basically, the parties to the dispute go into a room and aren't allowed to come back *out* of that room until an agreement has been reached.

Fortunately, nothing that dramatic is required where your cat is concerned. You may have heard just the opposite. Perhaps somebody once told you that cats are stubborn, unreasonable creatures. That an aggrieved cat might slash your sofa, poop in your shoes, or keep you up with her yowling all night just to punish you for not letting her get her own way.

Allow me to assure you that nothing could be further from the truth.

Whether you're haggling over a change in feeding schedule (*Pretty please, Socks, no more 5:00 am breakfasts...*), trying to wangle more time in the comfiest living room easy chair (*C'mon, Snowball—can't I just sit here during* NCIS?), or attempting to retain the entirety of your freshly made tuna sandwich, *any* cat can be negotiated with—quickly and decisively—by following this simple, two-step procedure:

Step 1: Give your cat whatever she wants.

Step 2: End negotiation.

See? Easy, peasy, **PAWSOME**!

Cats' toes look like beans

T hey're toes! But, somehow, also beans!

PAWSOME!

Cats never abandon you during the tough times

Whoever said, *Laugh and the world laughs with you, cry and you cry alone,* clearly never lived with a cat.

Inevitably in life there will be dark days—days when it feels as if even the people you love most have betrayed you or disappeared altogether. Days when all the news is bad and nobody will return your calls. Days when it feels as if there isn't a single friendly face anywhere to be found.

But if you live with a cat, you never have to look far.

Dogs have a well-deserved reputation for loyalty, which nobody in their right mind would try to dispute. But I always find the loyalty of cats to be more remarkable. Dogs are more naturally "hardwired" for group ties, for starters, whereas cats are solitary hunters who spook easily and dislike having their habits altered. And yet they've consented to live in our company, to put up with the sounds of televisions and garbage disposals and cars racing by outside. They stick by us when we move homes, get married, have babies, bring home more cats or even (gasp!) puppies to invade their territory.

And let's face it—for all the guff we give cats for being "mysterious" and "difficult" creatures to live with—it's not as if, from a cat's perspective, we're so easy to predict or figure out ourselves.

We don't necessarily make it easy for them, is what I'm saying.

Nevertheless, they stick by us. They might get anxious at times—and they'll certainly let us know when they do!—but they continue to purr right alongside us whether our paychecks rise or fall, our families grow or shrink, our surroundings become fancier or shabbier with the passage of years. Even on days when you hear a disheartening round of, "I'd *love* to be there for you if only I could..." your cat will be a rock-solid presence by your side.

No matter what.

Nowhere else will you find so much unconditional love and loyalty wrapped up in such a fuzzy, adorable, purring little package.

A cat's unwavering loyalty is about as **PAWSOME** as it gets.

Cats bring a touch of the wild into our lives

A *re cats domesticated?* is one of the most frequently Googled questions about cats—at least, judging by Google's autocomplete suggestions. Which implies that, as much as we typically think of cats as being "domestic" animals, deep down we're not *entirely* sure they are.

That ambivalence probably reflects a certain amount of truth. A growing body of evidence suggests that humans didn't so much domesticate cats as cats began to domesticate themselves—availing themselves of the abundant rodents we attracted when we invented farming—around 10,000 years ago (which sounds like a long time, but is still only a fraction of the time that dogs, for example, have been domesticated). And cats didn't even start morphing into household companions who lived indoors with us—as opposed to in our barns or around our grain silos—until about two hundred years ago, which is when humans first began consciously breeding cats for certain traits. In contrast, we've been breeding dogs to be less wolf-like for 30,000 years or even longer, by some estimates.

This is all by way of saying that the sense you sometimes get—as you see your little "house panther" slinking about the living room, looking for all the world like an actual panther or bobcat shrunk down to lap-sized cuteness—that your cat is equal parts wild animal and house pet is probably accurate. Since cats have, quite literally, done more to train us to do *their* bidding than vice versa, there's only so much of their innate wildness that they've had, or wanted, to give up.

I recently asked my readers on Facebook what their favorite thing about living with a cat was. The answers ranged from *You expect me to pick just one?!!?* to *My cat loves me unconditionally.* And then there was one person who wrote this:

Having a murder-mitten equipped ninja running through the house who then suddenly decides he needs to snuggle in my lap.

So the next time you feel your life is too tame, too constrained, too stultifyingly predictable, make a mental note to spend more time with your cat.

She remembers where the wild things are—and, if you're lucky, she'll let you know, too.

PAWSOME!

Cats chase their own tails

C'mon, you've seen it. It's like your very own clown show on the living room floor. And the angrier they seem to be getting at their own tails, the funnier it is to us.

So futile. So goofy. So delightfully **PAWSOME!**

Cats will persuade you not to get too many house plants

It's been my general experience that cats and houseplants don't go super-well together (unless you're growing cat grass—in which case, carry on). Cats are apt to chew on and otherwise maul indoor flora, not to mention the occasional tendency to substitute potting soil for kitty litter. (Yikes!)

It's probably just as well though because, honestly...did you really *want* all those houseplants, anyway?

People will warn you about all the inconveniences involved in adopting any kind of animal companion—the vet bills! the all-weather walks!—but they very rarely warn you about the burdens of keeping plants in your home.

Plants, I've come to learn, are *much* fussier about precise climate control then cats (which is saying something). And it's not like you can just put down a bowl of water and let the plant lap some up whenever it's thirsty—you have to *constantly* be aware of when *this* plant needs to be watered, and when *that* plant needs to be watered, and it's a sure bet that your various plants will have vexingly varied watering needs that you'll have to commit to memory. And when you leave town, forget about it! What friend will be stalwart enough to agree—without any arm-twisting, mind you—to come to your house every day and wade through an entire legal pad's worth of specific instructions regarding each individual plant's daily water intake and sun requirements?

And then there are the studies that say your plants won't grow properly if you don't talk to them all the time. Seriously? Most days I barely even feel like talking to the actual *humans* I know, and now I have to rattle my weary brain at the end of a long workday so I can dredge up appropriate conversational topics for a *houseplant?! Are you <u>kidding</u> me?!!?* Whose genius idea was this?!!?

At least cats are sensible enough to keep growing whether or not you natter nonsense at them all the livelong day..

In conclusion: You're soooooooooooo much better off having cats than lots of houseplants. There's just nothing **PAWSOME** about a home so strewn with vegetation, it looks like an abandoned *Tarzan* set.

Cats help you break in new furniture

There's nothing better, after years of living with the same old junk, than finally treating yourself to a brand-new sofa or recliner. Maybe you spend hours poring over catalogues or driving from store to store on your day off, searching for that one perfect piece that's *so* striking and *so* comfy, you say to yourself, "Here's something I'll be happy to look at and lie on, every day, for the next ten years."

The only problem, once the store's delivery guy has come and gone, is that everything else in your living room suddenly looks so shabby by comparison. Did that divan always list to one side? Was the wood on that coffee table always so dull and scratched up?

Not to worry, though—your cat has you covered! Just give Tabby the Interior-Decorator Cat one week of *fur*ee reign, and soon enough that brand-new addition to your living room will be adorned with a few tasteful claw marks and strategically placed patches of fur.

Not enough to make it look *worn out*, of course. Heavens no! Juuuuuuuust a few thoughtful little touches here and there to make the newcomer blend in seamlessly with the old.

And you won't even have to pay the outrageous rates a professional decorator would demand. Your cat will do the whole job for free—give or take the occasional handful of Greenies.

And that's because your cat is **PAWSOME!**

You can confess absolutely anything to your cat

Loved ones are apt to say, "Nothing you could say would change how I feel about you," but that's probably not strictly true. If, for example, you were to confess to even half your homicidal thoughts following a needlessly and excruciatingly prolonged one-on-one with your boss, you might find yourself squicking others out just a wee bit. Or if your spouse were to call home while away on a business trip to see what you were up to, and you replied, "Oh, you know...sitting around in my underwear eating chocolate chip cookie dough out of the tube," I very much fear that their high opinion of you might, inevitably, be a bit tarnished.

Your cat, on the other hand, has no flying figs to give when it comes to such confessions. I mean, let's face it—eating cookie dough straight out of the tube is still a more productive use of time than about ninety-nine percent of what your cat does all day. And why should homicidal fantasies trouble him when he *actually* killed two rats only a week ago *in real life?* "I did it for fun," your cat would probably tell you, cool as cucumber. "I wasn't even hungry." And while, with very few exceptions, a rat isn't a human being, your cat is probably unwilling to grant that people generally—with the very specific exception of *you*, of course—are all that much more sacred or special than any other type of creature.

The point is, your cat has an unshakeable belief that *you* are among the greatest and most exceptional of human beings ever to walk the earth. What other creature—on four legs or two—could dispense 'nip, treats, or love as well and freely as you do? And, given how exceptionally exceptional you are, what could you possibly confess to your cat that would change his opinion of you one iota?

Not to mention that he probably wouldn't understand most of whatever shameful secret you would admit to him, anyway. My own cats know their names, and the word "lunch," and beyond that it's strictly about facial expressions and tone of voice. "Yes, mommy *did* throw away household garbage in the dumpster behind the grocery store, even though *technically* it's against the law," I might say to them brightly—while administering behind-the-ears scritches, of course—and my cats' sole response would be to purr and gaze at me with the heavy-lidded eyes of feline adoration.

There aren't many relationships in life that will remain one hundred percent rock solid no matter what you confess to. But if you're owned by a cat, then you definitely have at least one.

And that's **PAWSOME!**

Cats meow, mew, coo, chitter, chatter, and whine

L eonardo da Vinci famously said that the smallest feline is a masterpiece.

I'd add that each and every cat is also a symphony—a full-fledged feline orchestra of one, with enough vocal range and differentiation to maintain a running, delightful conversation over the course of a lifetime.

The best part is that no two cats sound exactly alike.

Here, in no particular order, is a partial list of sounds I've observed my cats making over the years, along with an approximate guess-timation as to what each means:

Trill: *Yay! You're about to feed me!*

Chitter: *I would be killing those birds SO HARD if only this stupid window wasn't in the way!*

Coo: *I'm jumping onto the bed/onto the couch/into your lap right now!*

Chatter: *I have something VERY important to tell you. Most likely, it's a report of something you've done wrong—like not feeding me on time. I don't enjoy "scolding" you like this, but it's the only way you'll learn.*

Whine: *You're noooooooooot paying attention to meeeeeeeeeeeeeeeeeeeee!*

Mew: *I was sleeping and you woke me; or I want you to pay atten-*

tion to me; or *Gosh, that food you're eating looks yummy!*

Meow: *I'm irritated; I'm hungry; I want attention; You're talking to me, and I'm talking back; You're* not *talking to me, but I wish you would; Pet me; You're not petting me; You're STILL not petting me! I'm booooooooooored; You're home! I'm so happy to see you! Feed me now; No, seriously, feed me now...*

Pro tip: Be sure to record your cat now; someday you'll be able to play it back and say, "Remember the cute way Muffin used to ask me to pet her? That was **PAWSOME!**"

Cats teach us the importance of holding out for what we really want

Your cat has definite views on everything—not just *some* things, but *every*thing—from the type of food she prefers, to the exact brand of litter she requires, what does (and most certainly does *not*) constitute an acceptable sleeping surface, toys that rock and toys that blow, visitors to your home who are worth her time and those who are *persona non grata*, whether or not you should keep wearing that new perfume you just bought, and also…

It's a list that could go on at some length and encompass all that finds its way before your cat's judgmental eyes.

Suffice it to say that your cat is opinionated. *Very* opinionated.

What's more, she'd rather go hungry, or sleep standing up, or hold her bladder for hours, or be without company for days on end, than bend her exacting standards by even a fraction of an inch.

Don't get me wrong—there's something to be said for not being *too* rigid. A complete unwillingness to compromise is a difficult (not to mention lonely) way to go through life.

By the same token, doesn't it sometimes seem as if we're willing to give up on what we *really* want—and settle for what we secretly believe to be a substandard compromise—a little too easily? Why else would self-help be a billion-dollar industry, based on little more than teaching people how to be more assertive and find the confidence to demand what they truly desire, not just what they'll settle for?

Luckily for you, when it comes to things like being assertive and sticking to your guns, your cat is a certifiable expert—and would be fully willing to enlighten you by example for the entirely reasonable fee of a can of Fancy Feast.

PAWSOME!

Cats help us keep calm and carry on

Our cats entertain us, they soothe us, and they lull us to sleep with their purrs. They gambol about for our amusement, and they wreak havoc among our framed photos and glass tchotchkes for their own. Yet who could possibly stay mad at them when they look at us with so much love in their eyes?

The reason our cats can look at us with such love and perfect trust, even when things are at their absolute worst, is because they know one great truth—a truth we humans also know, although sometimes we forget that we do:

This too shall pass.

And when it does, things will be **PAWSOME**.

Eventually, we have to say goodbye to them

T he late comedian George Carlin once said that every pet is a tiny tragedy waiting to happen. By this, of course, he meant that eventually the day comes—far sooner than we're ready to—when we have to say goodbye.

It's inevitable that all of us cat lovers have moments, over the course of a long life lived with feline companions, when we wish all the way down to our souls that our cats could live as long as we do. While cats actually do live a relatively long time for house pets (and a few years longer than dogs typically do), that fifteen-year average lifespan could double, or even triple, and we wouldn't complain.

I don't want to work too hard to try to spin a negative into a positive. But when I think back on the cats I've been lucky enough to count among my family members, I'm struck by the fact that I was with them when they were teeny-tiny kittens, no more than a few weeks old, and I was also with them in their very last moments of life. And I do find something indescribably beautiful in this cradle-to-grave relationship—something wholly unique, unlike any other we get to have. In no other scenario do we get to see someone through all their firsts in life—perhaps even bottle-feeding them—and also be the one who has the enormous privilege of seeing them off as they breathe their last.

And even for those cats we adopt when they're a bit further along in their life cycle—the opportunity to see them through old age and its aftermath is as filled with warmth, comfort, and love as any sacred responsibility could possibly be.

Almost nothing has ever been harder for me than saying goodbye to the cats I've loved. Nevertheless, my last moments with each of them have been among the most beautiful of my life. I wouldn't trade them—or the memories of them I have today—for anything else in the world.

Perhaps it's the knowledge that our days with our feline companions are always numbered that makes these relationships as magical as they are. There are so many relationships that we take for granted, because deep down we know (or we *think* we know) that we'll have years and years in which to say the things we want to say, or to do the things we want to do together. We'll get in a fight with someone we love and then put off the tendering of apologies, secure in the woefully misguided belief that time is on our side.

The relative brevity of our time with our cats is a drawback, but it's also a gift. It's a reminder that the number of our days here on this earth are, in the end, finite and few.

Which means we have an obligation to make each and every day as **PAWSOME** as we possibly can!

Cats make us better humans

I was walking through an airport gift shop, a few years back, when I caught sight of a greeting card on a display rack that accomplished something no other greeting card I've seen before or since has ever managed to do: It stopped me dead in my tracks. It was a fairly simple card—nothing too fancy or "clever" about it. Beneath a beautiful illustration of a calico cat was the following inscription:

Be The Person Your Cat Thinks You Are.

I bought that greeting card instantly, and to this day I still have it hanging, in a little frame, on the wall above my desk.

We all joke about our cats thinking of us as "servants" or "staff," or regarding us as being incompetent in various ways—particularly when it comes to picking out toys or cat beds that they'll prefer to the bags and boxes said items came in. (*As if a mere human could ever comprehend the twists and turns of the feline mind!*)

But there's a version of me that only my cats see, and I know that it's the best possible version of myself. And while the actual me doesn't always line up with that best-possible me that glows in my cats' eyes, I do find that my cats tend to bring out the best I have to offer.

And while I couldn't say that my relationships with my cats are *better than* my relationships with other people, I will say that experiencing such easy and uncomplicated love—a respite from the more complex, and occasionally bruising, relationships I have with other people—has been a balm on my soul and one of the great joys of my life. And I think (at least, I hope) that I'm a better person for it.

I may never fully succeed in being quite the person my cat think I am. But, thanks to my cat, I do aspire to be a little bit better—and a little more **PAWSOME**—each and every day.

YOU ARE
PAWSOME!

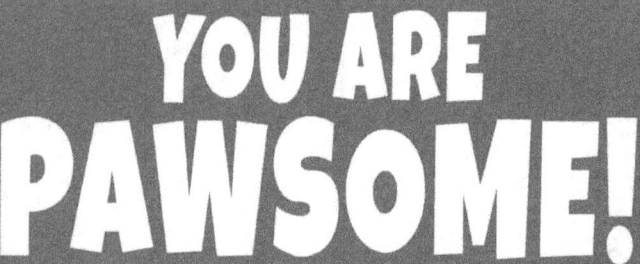

75 REASONS WHY YOUR CATS LOVE YOU, AND WHY LOVING THEM BACK MAKES YOU A BETTER HUMAN

GWEN COOPER

NEW YORK TIMES BESTSELLING AUTHOR OF HOMER'S ODYSSEY

Contents

Foreword

C onsider this book my open love letter to all the cat people out there—people who are, in my own humble opinion, some of the very greatest humans alive.

Cat lovers tend to get a bad rap—"crazy cat lady" being among the most common pejoratives routinely flung at us—which I'm inclined to chalk up to the pure jealousy others feel upon observing some of the more admirable qualities our cats routinely bring out in us and then burnish to a high gloss: patience, generosity of spirit, the ability to love unselfishly without expecting "rewards," and our willingness to engage even our non-human companions with a spirit of mutual respect and understanding.

The aloofness our cats sometimes display makes us more open. Their innate snobbishness keeps us from believing ourselves to be *their* superiors and makes us all the more humble. Their inscrutability makes us smarter, master detectives skilled in the reading of nuance.

They also make us far more appreciative of the little things in life—of those small moments of grace that can infuse even ordinary of days with something akin to magic: the tiny paw laid gently atop our own hand; the affectionate brush of a tail against our shins; the sound of a soothing purr against our heart as we drift off to sleep.

Not to mention that cats—being nature's funniest animals, hands down—instill in us a wicked sense of humor.

Don't believe me? Keep reading. This book is chock-full of examples proving that cat lovers are indisputably, irrefutably, and one-hundred-and-one percent totally

PAWSOME!

You clean the litter box

There's no end to how feline-besotted the genuine cat lover is. So besotted that a true devotee can find the positive spin on even the most negative aspects of cat care—the extra expense of a home-visiting pet-sitter when you travel ("Totally worth it!"); the always-dicey experience of pilling a cat ("Muffy looks so cute wrapped in a 'kitty burrito!'"); and even cleaning up hairballs ("Bootsie and I *love* the smell of Nature's Miracle!").

But the one un-spinnable negative is cleaning out the litter box. Probably the best that can be said is that, under certain ideal circumstances—including use of a high-quality litter, and making sure not too much time has passed since the last cleaning—it's relatively painless.

Then there are those *other* times. You know what I'm talking about. Those times when the store was out of your favorite litter, so you had to make do with some cheap substitute that doesn't even *pretend* to cover up the odor, which probably explains why you waited a couple of days longer than usual to clean it out...

And now here it is, the middle of summer, 95 degrees outside and even hotter than that *inside*, the sweltering heat and cheap litter having caused the odor coming from the litter box to mutate into some hideous, nearly tangible, practically paranormal entity that surely no cat—certainly not *your* cat, who's so cute and tiny!—could possibly be responsible for. Suddenly you're Marlon Brando at the end of *Apocalypse Now*, helplessly repeating the only semi-coherent thought your mind is capable of forming:

The horror! The horror!

In the end, though, you roll up your sleeves, clothespin your nose, grab the scooper and a plastic bag, and head in there to do what you have to do like the brave, never-say-die soldier you are.

Because when the going gets tough, the tough get

PAWSOME!

You're kind to other cats

I t's an absolute given that *your* cat—the cat who's snuggled up to you right now—is the all-time greatest cat that has ever lived or will ever live at any place or time in the entire history of the world, forever and ever, amen.

You're especially likely to feel this way if you're someone who, in your young and misguided years, swore up and down that you didn't particularly like cats, and couldn't see what all the fuss was about—and yet you somehow ended up living with a cat eventually (perhaps when a cat-owning romantic partner moved in), at which point you fell like one of the pens your new feline friend delighted in pushing off counters, devolving into a cooing, crooning, *who's my mushy kitty???* fool.

But even if you think of yourself as a one-cat human, it's inevitable that the love of one cat will lead you to cast a kindlier eye on other cats as well. You may one day find yourself setting out a bowl of kibble to feed a hungry-looking neighborhood cat you previously wouldn't have thought twice about. You'll almost certainly end up giving an affectionate scritch to the friend's cat—wending his way around your ankles when you drop by for a visit—who, once upon a time, you would have completely ignored.

The point is that there's something about loving *a* cat that leads to loving *all* cats.

This means that loving a cat makes your heart grow larger. And everybody knows that having a bigger heart makes you a kinder and all-around better human being.

Just like we claimed right on the cover of this very book!

PAWSOME!

You're kind of a sucker, in the best possible way

They say that a sucker is born every minute. And the day *you* were born was a red-letter day in the history of sucker-dom.

Of *course* you're a sucker. You're one of the biggest suckers going! It takes little more than a hang-dog (or hang-*cat*) expression before you're feeding your own dinner to one of your pampered felines, or allowing him to continue his comfy snooze on your very favorite sweater, or pausing a movie just at that pivotal moment when the killer's about to be revealed so you can fish out the toy your now-crying kitty accidentally pushed under the sofa.

You keep a stash of treats in hiding places throughout the house so they're always close at hand, just in case a sweet and imploring tug of a paw against your pant-leg makes it clear that a treat must be dispensed right *now*. You move your cat's bed from place to place in your living room over the course of the day, so that it's always ideally situated in the sunniest spot. You might make your spouse and kids eat a dinner they're not overly thrilled with—but if the latest can you put down for Buttons is clearly bumming him out, a new and different flavor is never far behind.

In other words, you're a rube. It's no secret that your (kind of a) con-artist cat manages to bamboozle you daily with the greatest of ease.

When pressed on the subject, there's nothing you can do but admit it. Maybe it's all true. Maybe you actually *are* one of the biggest suckers who ever lived.

But as long as we're truth-telling—isn't that really just another way of saying you have a heart as big as all outdoors?

PAWSOME!

You let your cat lie on top of you

It could be 100 degrees outside. You could be full to bursting with that half (whole?) pizza you just consumed while re-watching Season 4 of *Game of Thrones* (#JusticeForSerPounce). Your cat could be a 25-lb. Maine Coon whose weight is a challenge for you to support, even under ideal circumstances.

No matter what, though—if Queeney wants to lie on your belly, then that's exactly what you're going to let Queeney do.

Is it uncomfortable? You betcha! But what's a little discomfort between very best friends?

And besides, it's incredibly flattering to know that your cat literally can't get close enough to you.

PAWSOME!

You open doors for your cat
(and close them...and open them...)

What is it with cats and doors? My own cats have never met a closed door they could abide—even if that closed door leads into a room they have no desire to enter, or out of a room they have no desire to leave.

Capriciousness, thy name is cat.

There are any number of theories as to why cats abhor a closed door even more than nature supposedly abhors a vacuum. (Come to think of it, my cats aren't especially fond of the vacuum, either.) These include separation anxiety—the idea that your cat simply can't bear to be parted from you—a fear of being trapped in a room and at the mercy of potential predators when the door is closed, plain old curiosity (*say...what's behind that closed door anyway???*), and the maddeningly circular theory that states we've trained our cats to cry whenever they see a closed door by opening that door for them whenever they cry.

Heh.

I think we all know it's actually the other way around—that it's our cats who've trained *us* to do their bidding, and that when they demand we open a closed door or close an open door, they're simply exercising the prerogative that all masters have over their servants, i.e. the right to make arbitrary demands at all times and for no particular reason.

And while I'm not one to generally advocate for vassalage as a desirable state, I will say that acceding to my cats' more unreasonable demands with a kind of automatic patience has made me much more patient when, for instance, I'm filling out complicated health insurance forms, or dealing with an unreasonable desk clerk down at the DMV.

PAWSOME!

You read around your cat

A nd what is it with cats and newspapers?

Or cats and magazines?

Or cats and that book you have opened in front of you?

I used to have a hypothesis that your cat would see your eyes glued to a page and think something like, *There is NO WAY I'm letting her look at that magazine instead of at me!*, and would therefore resolve to get between *you* and *it* so as to effectively hijack your attention.

It was a good-enough theory, as such things go. But then I adopted a blind cat who very obviously couldn't see where my eyes were looking at any given moment (and didn't even have a working understanding of things like "eyes" and "looking"), and my blind cat *also* would instantly sprawl atop any magazine, newspaper, book, et cetera that I might have spread out on the table or floor before me.

Which means there's probably just something irresistible about the sensation of paper under their furry bellies that has your cats entranced.

Sure, you've been known to unceremoniously shove your cat off a book or newspaper so you can continue reading. But if you're anything like me (a born sucker, no doubt about it), you're just as apt to ask yourself, *Is there _really_ anything entertaining and/or informative enough in these pages to justify disturbing Tabby when she's so comfy?*

And, after concluding that there almost certainly isn't, you content yourself with whatever fragments of sentences or paragraphs are visible around Tabby's fuzzy tummy—all the while assuring yourself that the sacrifice of reading material is a trifling thing when compared to the comfort of your beloved feline.

PAWSOME!

You work around your cat

While we're on the subject—what is it about cats and computers?

Or cats and desks?

Or cats and desk *chairs*?

Or cats and...well, you see where I'm going with this.

If it's something that's adjacent or essential to your work—something without which your work couldn't get done—there's a reasonably high chance your cat will be utterly fascinated by it.

Of course it's perfectly adorable and all that. But it doesn't change the fact that attempting to type on a keyboard that currently has a cat dancing up and down its keys—trying mightily to add her own imprint to your work reports by inserting an emphatic ***ad;lskfahk;h!*** for flourish—can make the actual *work* of getting your work done vexing, to say the least.

Look, you wouldn't be human if you didn't, on occasion, simply shoo your cat well clear of your workspace and get back down to business.

But you're probably just as apt to find yourself typing with a face-full of fur, hands spaced awkwardly on your keyboard as you try to edge around your cat's flapping tail to get a decent look at the screen in front of you.

That's because you're flexible, dexterous, and capable of effective multitasking. And also because nothing in your hierarchy of values—not even your work—comes ahead of your cat.

PAWSOME!

You sleep around your cat

It's an immutable law of physics that even a small, five-pound cat is somehow capable of taking up roughly the same amount of space in a bed as a six-foot-two, two-hundred-fifty-pound man.

I don't know how they manage it, either. As with so many things when it comes to cats, it's a mystery!

What isn't a mystery is why you choose to contort your body into pretzel-like formations that would be the envy of a Cirque du Soleil performer rather than kick Milo out of bed, or even so much as disturb his slumber.

You do it because, when it comes to your cats, you will *literally* give 'til it hurts. And being a giver is

PAWSOME!

In games of cat and mouse, you're always "mouse"

When it comes to playing "cat and mouse," the rules are simple and exactly the same as the outcome, which is predetermined.

To wit: The cat gets the mouse.

The mouse is the eternal dupe of Fate, destined to be forever pounced upon. No matter how favorable the odds may appear at first, the deck is always stacked against him. Any hope that *this* face-off against the cat might be different is nothing more than a mirage floating on the horizon.

And yet, you always take the mouse role when playing a spirited game with your cat, wiggling fingers and toes under blankets or tablecloths or t-shirts or whatever else is handy. Never once is the game reversed. Never once, say, does your cat casually stroll past a bed *you're* hiding beneath, where *you* wait to leap out and pounce upon *him*.

And even as your poor digits are bruised and torn for the umpteenth time by the teeth and claws of sweet little Fluffy, you smile courageously and remind yourself—even as your cat is using parts of your body as his own personal chew toys—that love and self-sacrifice are practically the same thing.

"It is a far, far more **PAWSOME** thing that I do than I have ever done..."

You berate yourself whenever you scold your cat

My cats are certifiable experts at making me feel guilty—although, given that I'll feel crushing guilt all on my own for forgetting to order a pizza with a well-done crust (my husband's preference), or for disturbing the robins and squirrels when I hang out in my back yard, making *me* feel guilty is clearly so easy as to be unworthy of my cats' prodigious talents. No need for them to open their eyes wide in a hangdog expression, or rub harder than usual against my leg in an attempt to remind me that their breakfast really *should* have been served twenty minutes ago. (*What kind of a monster makes helpless cats wait twenty minutes to be fed???*)

The worst, however, is when I find myself having to scold my cats for one reason or another—Clayton for having chewed the ear off of the cat-shaped wooden footrest I once brought home from a flea market. (Clayton likes to chew wood. Yeah...I don't get it, either.) Or Fanny for having pilfered a sample bag of dry kibble from the kitchen cabinet she *knows* she's not allowed to open.

Bad cat! I'll say in the sternest voice I can muster, accompanied by an equally stern wag of my finger. *That's very, very bad!*

But then, inevitably, I feel like an ogre. *They didn't* <u>*mean*</u> *to be bad,* I remind myself. *They're just doing what cats do.* Who do I think I am, anyway—the matron of some dour reform school for misbehaved cats? What do my poor kitties even have to look forward to in their listless little days, if not for whatever love and affection

I dole out to them? Without that, their lives would be nothing but an endless, joyless cycle of naps and toys and back rubs, and thoughtfully prepared meals served punctually on time.

Quelle horreur! Who could endure such an existence?!

It's usually when I reach this point in my thoughts—and as a way of offsetting the intensity of my guilt—that I'll haul out the Temptations bag and dispense treats with a liberal hand. *Forgive me for having yelled at you!* I plead. *I didn't mean it! I'll do better next time!*

The irony of the whole thing is that—as their bored little faces are at pains to remind me—my cats, being cats, never actually gave a flip that I was angry at them in the first place.

PAWSOME!

You always put food in the bowl

Your cat might obsess over seemingly negligible taste differences between his favorite cat-food brand's Shredded Chicken Dinner (yum!) and their Minced Chicken Dinner (yuck!). Or maybe get incredibly fussy about another flavor of food he scarfed down with wild enthusiasm as recently as yesterday. Maybe even—heaven forfend!—you might oversleep one morning or get home late from work one evening, forcing your cat to wait a whole half-hour longer for his morning or evening repast than he's accustomed to waiting.

Bottom line, though? Your cat knows you're going to put *something* edible in that bowl Every. Damn. Day.

Even when the prices of gas and milk and bread and oranges rise to outrageous heights. Even when that year-end bonus your boss promised fails to materialize. Even when you lose your job altogether and have to resort to eating mayonnaise sandwiches without the mayonnaise. Come hell or high water, your cat has never once gone hungry.

Because you're reliable. Because you're *rugged*. Because you're **PAWSOME!**

You give your cat adorable nicknames

C ats have their cat-specific rituals of inclusion—things like head-bonking, touching noses, and scent-marking your ankles. We humans have our own ways of letting the world know that our cats are family members, like including them in family photo portraits, getting a tattoo that features a cat's name or likeness, or writing our cats into our wills. (You may laugh, but do you know who would take your moggy in if something were to happen to you?)

For my money, though, one of the very best ways of letting your cats know they're equally valued family members is with the bestowing of a "family only" nickname.

My own cats have their real names, of course—the ones that go on their medical records and travel documents. But then there are the names known only to family and close friends. Clayton, for example, is known as Clayton, aka The Clayman, aka Claymation, aka "Littleman" (a running together of "little man," which somehow became a *thing* in our house when, after years of referring to Clayton as "my mushy little man," my husband decided to make the two words into a single surname-like nickname.)

And then there's his sister Fanny, aka Fandemonium, aka Fanny-cat, aka Fan-Fan, aka Miss Fanny Pants (I think I was originally going for a "fancy-pants" riff).

I won't share the family-only names my husband and I have for each other. Suffice it to say that everyone in our house—four-legged and two—has at least one nickname known only to those who reside within these four walls, and never uttered in front of outsiders.

Just like in your house! Which is how your cats know 100% for sure that they're completely official, much-beloved, fully vested members of the only club they're likely ever to think it worth their while to join.

PAWSOME!

You sing your cat silly love songs

D id you know that the word "kitty" can be substituted for the word "baby" in just about any song?

This is true in general, but particularly in the case of Motown classics, a happy happenstance I was thinking about just the other day while warbling an off-key rendition of The Miracles' "Ooo Kitty Kitty."

Who, for example, can refrain from crooning along with Martin Gaye's "Too Busy Thinking About My Kitty"? Or The Shirelles' "Kitty It's You"? I've been known to murder an interpretation of The Supremes' hit "Kitty Love" at dubiously appropriate times.

When it comes to my absolute favorite, though, it's a two-way tie between Ronnie Spector and The Ronnettes' "Be My Kitty" and "Kitty I Love You." (*Have I ever told you/ How good it feels to hold you?*)

Not that it ultimately matters what specific song you're singing to your rapt feline audience of one. The important thing is that your cat knows you're singing for him, and him alone.

Bonus points for working your cat's name into "The Name Game"! (*Patches, Patches, Bo-batches, bonana fanna fo-fatches...*)

PAWSOME!

You give your cat daily massages

A recent lower-back spasm was of such agonizing intensity that I found myself unable even to hobble as far as the nearest chiropractor—and so, for the first time in my life, I hired a massage therapist to come to my home.

My tripod cat, Clayton, stayed pretty close while the massage was going on—Clayton being a very "present" cat—and the massage therapist, a cat lover herself, remarked that he was clearly one of those cats who likes to "supervise" the humans around him.

That may very well be, but my suspicion is that Clayton wasn't trying to exercise his cat's prerogative of being in charge of all the people around him.

He was trying to figure out why *I* was the one getting the massage instead of *him.*

After all, a full-body rubdown is a cherished part of Clayton's daily ritual. If more than 24 hours passed without soothing, scratching fingers all down the length of his back, he'd surely feel that he'd been monstrously deprived.

Some people may have cats that like to "groom" them, as my cats occasionally do for me. But let's be honest: Most cats will simply accept your daily ministrations—the scratching, the rubbing, the massages—as no more than their due.

And you, upon seeing (and hearing!) your cat's purring pleasure—and even though you're on the giving rather than the receiving end of all this attention—are still likely to think that you're the one getting the better end of the deal.

PAWSOME!

You don't make your cat feel weird about being weird

I t always gets my back up when I hear some non-cat person talking about how "weird" cats are. Scoop out a few litter-boxes and pay your dues like the rest of us, and then maybe—*maybe*—you'll be entitled to opine on the alleged "weirdness" of cats.

Since we're just talking amongst ourselves, though, we can be honest and admit it: Cats are kinda weird. They get all riled up for no apparent reason and chase invisible things up the walls and sleep in boxes that are WAY too small to be comfortable and chitter at birds outside and run away at top speed from their own poop like pooping was a crime and they're barely one step ahead of johnny law.

Those of us who love cats, however, know that variety is the spice of life. Truth be told, many of us are a bit on the odd side ourselves, which is why we actually like the "weirdness" in our cats.

In fact, we don't just like it—we love it! We love that each and every one of our cats has their own individual quirk, like only being willing to drink water out of *our* water glass, or leaving the same stuffed mouse on our pillow every night, or *constantly* showing us their butt. (Actually, that last one probably applies to all cats.)

Nobody ever attained greatness by being just like everybody else. And let me ask you this: Do you love the ones you love because they're so ordinary, or do you love them for the ways in which they're different and unique and stand out from the crowd?

Wouldn't it, in fact, be fair to say that noticing those differences in someone else is how love usually begins? And wouldn't it *also* be fair to say, then, that those of us who already have a propensity for appreciating a little bit of weirdness—the whole reason why we love our cats in the first place!—are somewhat likelier to be kind and accepting of others, even (and especially!) if they're slightly on the odd side?

So there you have it: We embrace the weirdness in our cats without ever doing anything to squelch their unique personalities or make them feel self-conscious. We savor their little eccentricities through the eyes of a connoisseur, not the eyes of a conformist.

And it's exactly this tendency that makes us more loving, more open-hearted, and more accepting human beings in general.

PAWSOME!

You defend your cat against visitors who complain about cat hair

What's a cat-hating psychopath like *that* even doing in your house in the first place???
PAWSOME!

You find your cat's bloodlust adorable

If you had a relative or coworker who was always thinking about the violent murder of bunnies and songbirds, chances are you'd find that person kind of...icky. *I guess he* probably *won't murder me and stuff my corpse in a Dumpster*, you'd reassure yourself, right before asking HR to reassign you to some faraway cubicle, or scratching Cousin Creepy off the invite list for your wedding.

Personally, I'm a big fan of the various birds, bunnies, squirrels, butterflies, opossums, and other wildlife denizens who populate my back yard. I throw out nuts and seeds and little bits of bread on a regular basis, and I set out bowls of water when the weather is particularly dry. I had to wait nearly three months this year to get some much-needed professional yard work done—only to reschedule my long-awaited appointment when it finally arrived, because by then I had two little robin fledglings hopping around my back yard under the watchful eye of their *very* uptight mama, and the thought of their combined anxiety when faced with the deafening roar of weed whackers was enough to give *me* an anxiety attack.

I get a little over-invested in the birds and bunnies, is what I'm saying.

And yet, like the vast majority of cat-moms and dads, the sight of my cats crouched in front of the French doors that lead out to our back yard, every inch of their poise and posture proclaiming, *I was born to kill birds and bunnies, and that's just what I'm going to do*—tickles me to no end.

Who's mommy's little hunter? I croon fondly. *Who's my fuzzy-wuzzy wizzle attack kitty?*

I should probably add here that my cats are strictly indoor-only and have never even come close to killing a bird or a bunny—or anything else furry, winged, or crawling, with the exception of the occasional palmetto bug or housefly unfortunate enough to make it inside. The most my cats can do is watch with quivering haunches and full-black murder eyes from behind reinforced glass.

And while I would be absolutely horrified, were I to actually witness my beloved felines dispatching one of those fledgling robins I've become so emotionally invested in, seeing my cats tremble with the desire—and very clear intent—to do so inevitably leaves me shaking my head lovingly while murmuring an affectionate, *Awwwwwwww!* under my breath.

What can I say? I tend to love things for being what they are. I love the birds for flying and building their nests, the squirrels for scampering after nuts and eating breadcrumbs so daintily with their tiny paws, the opossum mama for carrying her wee babes in a row on her back...

And I love my own sweet little house panthers, who are nearly bursting with their insatiable desire to horribly, horribly murder each and every last one of them.

PAWSOME!

You sit in one position as long as humanly possible, just because your cat is comfy

I t's a scorching midsummer day and your air conditioner is broken. With each second that goes by, your legs are getting sweatier and sweatier beneath their burden of snoozing cat-flesh—not to mention more filled with pins and needles than a dressmaker's etui. (Crossword-ese for "pretty box that holds sewing stuff.")

Any rational person would have long-since shoved the sleepy kitty from their lap and stretched out their legs to restore blood circulation and air flow. Not you, though. You grit your teeth, mop your brow, declare that your only regret is having but one lap to dedicate to feline-kind, and then give that adorably fuzzy heat-bag on your legs an additional scritch under the chin for good measure.

Superman may be made of steel, but *you* are made of **PAWSOME**!

You talk to your cats like they can understand you

Sure, know-nothing strangers may find the running conversation you have with your cats deeply odd. After all, they'll point out oh-so-smugly, it's not like your cats understand what you're saying. And what's even the point of talking to someone who can't talk back?

Well, I'm not so sure that our cats can't understand what we're saying. (My cats have the uncanny ability to know when my husband and I are discussing dinner plans or vet appointments). And anyone who's spent enough time around cats—with their colorful range of meows, mews, chirps, chitters, and purrs—knows that cats have a *very* expressive language all their own.

But even if none of that were true, the bottom line is that your cats can certainly tell *when* you're saying something to them, even if they have no idea *what* you're saying. And, judging by the spirited mews and purrs with which they greet the sound of your voice, just being included in the conversation makes a cat feel good.

And isn't making somebody else feel good one of the very best reasons for doing anything at all?

Not that you need *me* to tell you that. Living with cats has already made you the kind of person who loves doing all the little things that make someone else happy—even if ignorant onlookers are incapable of seeing the value in it.

PAWSOME!

You refrain from rubbing your cat's belly

I f you're a cat lover (and, honestly, why wouldn't you be?), then you probably find kitty bellies well-nigh irresistible.

My own cat Fanny has a habit of rolling around seductively on her back, flashing her fuzzy underside until the cuteness of it is more than mortal flesh can bear…and then quickly contracting into a veritable Venus flytrap—claws and teeth snapping shut around my fingers—the instant they make contact with her tummy.

Cats, as a general rule, prefer not to have their bellies rubbed—a point they are more than willing to drive home with the kind of emphasis that often leaves ailurophiles reaching for the band-aids and rubbing alcohol.

The truly maddening thing is that cats are apt to roll over and display those fluffy, scrumptious, maddeningly rub-able undercarriages when they're at their most relaxed and trusting—in short, when your cat is about as adorable as the laws of physics will allow any living creature to be. The impulse to sink your fingers into that delectable fluff can be a sorer temptation than a warm brownie sundae after a month of dieting.

Nevertheless, knowing as you well do how irritating most moggies find it to have their bellies rubbed—and how giving cats such utterly enticing bellies, and then programming them to hate having those bellies even *touched*, is surely evidence that God enjoys practical jokes—you hold back. Your hands remain firmly in your pockets while the tantalizing little succubus who shares your home wriggles around on his back, blissfully unaware (or, perhaps, all *too* aware) of the agony he's inflicting on you.

You hold back because you have willpower. Because you respect the rights of this independent creature you live with and because, no matter how tempted you may be, you don't want to undermine his sense of security or autonomy by imposing your will on his own.

In other words: Because you're **PAWSOME!**

But sometimes you rub your cat's belly!

O f course, every so often you'll run across the unusual cat who actually *likes* having his tummy rubbed. My own Clayton is just such a cat—one who'll jump into my lap, promptly flip onto his back, and all but *demand* that I make with the belly rubs, posthaste.

 If you have a tummy-rub-loving cat, then you know what it's like to sit there in one spot, scritching away, as the evening news gives way to primetime and eventually melts into the late-night talk shows. Your hand grows as numb as your legs beneath the weight of your cat, while you forgo food, sleep, or even a slightly more comfortable sitting position.

All because your cat is purring so contentedly under your ministrations that you couldn't *possibly* bear to disturb him.

And also because you're **PAWSOME!**

You're the only one who understands what your cat is "saying"

C ats tend to develop their "vocabularies" around their own specific and unique concerns. My tripod cat Clayton has his "Throw my fetching toy!" meow. My cat Scarlett—a creature of rather fastidious habits—had a cry that meant "My litter box is not adequately clean!" And my blind cat, Homer—who had neither faith in, nor knowledge of, the many visual cues a cat can offer—had a rich and subtle vocabulary capable of conveying everything from, "Pay attention to me!" to "I want tuna, not turkey!" to "You're sleeping WAY too late!" (This last injunction—usually offered in the predawn darkness that a blind cat could perhaps be forgiven for not noticing—was always particularly mortifying.)

The thing is, though, it's not like there's any *universal* cat language that you, as a cat lover, could learn once and for all and then apply to every subsequent feline who pads through your life. Learning your specific cat's particular whims, fancies, and preferences takes real effort and patience—along with the commitment to someone else's peace of mind that only arises in the closest and most meaningful of relationships.

Although the way your cat would probably express it would be more like, "My human is *sooooooo* easy to train! That's why he's **PAWSOME!**"

You speak to your cats in that special voice that's just for them

E very "cat person" has a "cat voice." That silly-but-affectionate voice you only use when speaking directly to your cat—preferably when nobody else is around to hear it.

No two cat voices sound exactly alike. Your own might be high and squeaky or low and rumbly, or it might flow from between your lips with a spirited, sing-song cadence. Maybe you say perfectly coherent (if not exactly intelligent) things in your cat voice, like: "Who wants nom-noms? Do *you*? Do *you* want nom-noms?" Or perhaps you go full-unintelligible-babble with something like, "Whodaitsybitsyfuzzywizzlenomnomkitty???"

And maybe your cat, upon hearing this loveable nonsense, glows with the knowledge that she's being singled out as special. Maybe she even "talks" back to you with those specific mews or meows that you—and only you—are capable of interpreting correctly.

Maybe she simply rolls her eyes. Or whatever the feline equivalent of eye rolling is.

However it goes down, the one constant is that, for just that moment, your cat knows to a certainty that she's the sole focus of your attention—that you're not speaking to anybody else in the whole wide world except her.

And *you* get the satisfaction of knowing that you've made your beloved kitty feel just a little bit more beloved.

PAWSOME!

Sometimes you sit on the floor with your cat

C ats spend so much time on the floor—snoozing, scampering, rolling around on their backs in a puddle of sunlight—that it can be easy to forget how much time we humans *don't* spend on the floor.

Sure, we *walk* on the floor. But lying on the floor—without so much as a yoga mat for a cushion—is the pits. Sleeping on the floor is brutal torture. Even sitting on the floor isn't all that much fun, particularly as you get older and getting back up *off* the floor becomes a real challenge.

Maybe that's why your cat is so darn tickled on those occasions when you throw caution and comfort to the wind and hunker down on the tiles—or possibly even lie down and stretch out full length—just so your cat can have the joy of climbing, perching, burrowing, and snuggling all over you from his preferred floor-bound vantage point rather than on a chair, sofa, or bed like he's used to doing.

Those times when you actually join your kitty at floor level are a full-fledged special occasion. It's an instant *paw*ty, and it's pretty **PAWSOME!**

You brush your cats to get rid of dry skin and old fur

It keeps their fur from getting matted. It improves their circulation. And it feels sooooooooooooo good...
PAWSOME!

Doody-butt!!!

Maybe you call it something different in your house.

Maybe you don't have a name for it at all. Maybe you've never heard yourself, of a quiet Sunday morning, hollering to your husband who's downstairs making coffee, "Bring up some toilet paper! We've got a Category 5 doody-butt emergency!"

I'm referring, of course, to the unpleasant but well-nigh inevitable eventuality of having your cat step into the litterbox to do his business, then exit said litterbox having sadly failed to leave *everything* behind.

Sometimes your cat remains blissfully unaware of the problem. Sometimes he's *entirely* aware, scooting his hind-quarters frantically across white rugs and fresh bedsheets and assorted pieces of tough-to-clean furniture—or perhaps even (as my Clayton does) attempting to outrun the sticky stowaway, which is about as effective as trying to treat a headache with leeches.

Regardless, dollars to donuts your cat will both desperately need your help to resolve the matter, and also at the same time adamantly refuse to accept any help from you whatsoever.

Many's the time I've found myself, roll of toilet paper clutched in my hand, racing around the house after a fleeing cat—knowing that my eventual reward, when I finally do catch her, will be the joy of using said toilet paper to pull poop from her *tuchus* fur like I was trying to get peanut butter out of a shag rug.

Unpleasant as it is, however, when push comes to shove (comes to poop), you roll up our sleeves and get in there to handle the sticky situation like the champ you are.

Being a cat-parent ain't always glamorous, but that's the mother-flipping job.

PAWSOME!

You score weed for your cat

Y ou've never broken the law in your entire life.

Never so much as claimed an even slightly questionable tax deduction. Never sped through an "orange" traffic light. Never carved your sweetheart's name into a tree at the park or taken a chewed-up wad of gum out of your mouth and stuck it the underside of a desk.

When it comes to walking the straight-and-narrow, you could teach a Master Class.

Which is what makes it all the more surprising to onlookers (although not, I can assure you, to your fellow cat lovers) when you oh-so-casually walk in with an ounce of that wacky feline weed *nepeta cataria* (otherwise known as garden-variety catnip), sprinkle some around the floor, and watch as your cat proceeds to get as high as a Georgia pine.

PAWSOME!

You remember to turn off the flash so your cat doesn't get "laser eyes" in photos

O kay, so maybe you don't *always* remember to do this. And maybe your cat doesn't actually care about looking like she has "laser eyes" in photos. Maybe, if she could be made to understand what laser eyes were, she'd even think it was kinda cool. *It looks like my eyes are shooting lasers!* she'd say. *Badass!*

But *you* know that laser eyes tend to look doofy in a finished photo—not so much like your cat is a lethal warrior goddess, but more like she got caught unawares when you pointed the camera at her face, which makes her just as apt to have one of those unprepared, unflattering, open-mouthed, *derp* expressions that make the rest of us dread seeing candid photos of ourselves even more than we dread doing our taxes every year. (And I'm a freelancer, so that's, like, a *lot* of dread!)

The point is that you're the kind of person who looks out for others even when they're not looking out for themselves. And the way you do your level best to make sure your kitty looks just as adorable in every picture you snap of her as she does in the furry flesh is merely one more example of just how **PAWSOME** you are!

You let your cat have all the pillows

When you walk into your bedroom and see your cat asleep on the bed, sprawled out strategically so that some part of her body—one outstretched paw, perhaps, or the very tip of her tail—is at least slightly touching each and every pillow on the bed, do you shove her out of the way so that you can lie down yourself?

Or do you say *Awwwwwwwwww* and leave kitty to her luxurious slumber?

Yeah...that's what I thought. Ya big softy!

PAWSOME!

You let your cat sleep on clean clothes fresh from the dryer

I t can never be too hot for my cats—particularly Fanny, who's never happier than in the oppressive summertime heat of the sundrenched primary bedroom on the very top floor of our very old house (full of Victorian-era charm, but sadly *sans* central AC). Fanny likes to sprawl out full-length in the sweltering bedroom while snoozing contentedly in the biggest sun puddle she can find, soaking up the intense warmth until her coal-black fur feels like actual hot coals.

Unfortunately for Fanny, there are too many months in the year when the thermometer barely rises above freezing here in the Northeast—months when the angle of the sun is such that even the occasional sun puddle becomes a rare treat rather than a daily occurrence.

But on the plus side for Fanny—and for all those other heat-worshipping cats like her—there's always once-a-week laundry to look forward to, and the inevitable bag, basket, or pile of clean clothing fresh out of the dryer. Clothing that's still warm to the touch and thus an absolutely *purr*-fect spot for a not-so-quick catnap.

Of course, one of the main goals that a cat lover's weekly washing has to accomplish is the removal of cat fur from all the shirts, sheets, pants, towels, and so on where it tends to accumulate. Simple logic would therefore seem to dictate that allowing a cat to immediately lie all over that freshly de-furred clothing might be just a tad self-defeating.

But allow me to counter that seemingly flawless reasoning by asking a simple question: Is there anything more adorable on the whole face of the earth than the sight of a sweetly sleeping cat curled up smack-dab in the middle of a huge mound of clothing? And isn't it kind of worth doing all the work of sorting and cleaning and drying your clothes, just for this deeply gratifying sight?

After all, there's always the prospect of next week's laundry—and newly fur-free clothes—ahead of you. And, as a wise internet meme has pointed out, rich people may have designer labels on their clothing, but *happy* people have cat fur on theirs.

PAWSOME!

You bring Da Bird to life

A bunch of feathers glued to the end of a string that's glued to the end of a stick might not sound like an invention whose importance equals that of moving pictures, say, or the polio vaccine.

But as far as your cat is concerned, it's a concoction of sheer wizardry—and *you* are the only being advanced enough to bring it to magical life!

You make it dance and spin. You make it fly high in the air and then dip perilously close to crashing on the ground before it rebounds to hang just above your kitty's nose, tantalizing her nearly to the point of madness. In a good way.

It's just about her favorite game, aside from Biting Toes Under The Covers and Pushing Things Off The Table—except that in *this* game nothing gets bruised, cracked, or otherwise damaged, aside from maybe a cluster of feathers that was designed for that exact purpose.

And it's all thanks to *you*—your home's Imagineer in Chief.
PAWSOME!

You probably saved your cat's life when you adopted him

E very year in the U.S. alone, some six-point-three million companion animals end up in shelters.

Roughly half of those companion animals are cats. About one-third of those cats will eventually be euthanized. And that's not even counting the number of stray cats who would benefit enormously from living in loving homes—who, in many cases, have been abandoned by humans who once cared for them but then, one day, simply tossed them out—and who languish outside of the shelter system, but are no less desperate for it.

Which is why it's no exaggeration to say that you almost certainly saved your cat's life when you adopted him.

But even if you adopted your cat from a no-kill shelter—someplace that would have guaranteed your kitty a caring lifelong home even if you'd never swooped in to save the day—you've nevertheless still saved a life. By adopting one cat, you've opened up a much-needed space in that no-kill shelter for another cat to be saved.

I realize I'm leaving out cat-parents who may have obtained their beloved feline friends from a breeder. Although my own inclinations tend toward #adoptdontshop, I realize that ethical breeders play an important role in the cat-loving community. Love is love, after all, no matter how it ends up coming into our lives.

Still, the sheer number of rescue-cat adopters who swear up and down that "I didn't save her, *she* saved *me*!" should give you pause—and hopefully lead you to at least consider the possibility of adopting a rescue cat the next time around.

The life you save may be your own.

PAWSOME!

You let your cat follow you into the bathroom

I 've heard some ailurophiles say they have a closer and more intimate relationship with their cat than with their significant other.

If I'm being totally honest, I have to admit that—close as my husband and I are—there are any number of intimate things that my cats, and *only* my cats, will ever see me do. Some are of the goofy, dancing-around-the-house-in-your-underwear variety that you can't quite bring yourself to let anybody see. But most take place in that most private of private spaces, the *sanctum sanctorum* of every household.

I refer, of course, to the bathroom.

There are things I do in the bathroom that my husband has never seen and will never see (if there's any god at all). It's not that I worry my husband would love me less if he happened to see me sitting on the toilet or shaving my armpits. (Although seeing me do both simultaneously might take some of the bloom off the rose.)

It's just that I'd rather engage in these activities without any kind of an audience *at all*. And for that reason it took me a minute to adjust to having my cats with me in the bathroom—and, furthermore, to having a cat with me in the bathroom *at all times*, no matter what I happened to be doing.

My Vashti—the second cat I ever adopted—used to sit at my feet and watch with rapt attention as I applied makeup, and her successor, my current cat Fanny, enjoys doing so to this day. My clingy Clayton, unusually for a cat, never needs or wants any time alone, and seems to resent even the implication that I might desire five cat-free minutes in my day. In his old age, my cat Homer used to curl up atop the clothes hamper while I showered, and snooze peacefully in the warmth of the steam. *Like an old man taking a shvitz,* I would tell my husband.

Perhaps you also have an instinctive desire for strict bathroom privacy. But perhaps you, like me, find yourself wondering, *Is there really any good reason to lock my cats out? Especially when it seems to make them so happy to be in here?*

And that, as always, is the best and final argument.

How could you bring yourself to deny your cat those small moments of joy she appears to experience when sitting at your feet, looking up at you intently as you masque your face, or curl your eyelashes, or clasp that one errant chin hair firmly betwixt your tweezers and give it a good yank?

And it's not like there's anybody else who could sit there watching you do these things and *still* maintain a glow in their eyes that clearly says, *You're the most fascinating creature on the face of the earth!*

PAWSOME!

You don't stare at your cats, even when they stare at you

If cats could talk, this would be a classic, "Do as I say, not as I do," situation.

Actually, cats *do* kind of talk to us—with their varied meows, for example (indicating everything from "feed me now" to "that dog outside is scaring me!"), or with their posture and how they hold their tails.

And a cat who's staring straight at you is definitely trying to communicate something. Generally speaking, if your cat is staring at you, it should be interpreted as a sign of affection—especially if it's accompanied by a few slow blinks.

On the other hand, you should DEFINITELY not stare back at your cat! An unwavering, unblinking stare will be construed as a sign of aggression and will most likely get her literal and figurative back up.

In short, it's a bad idea to stare at your cat. But when your cat stares at *you*, on the other hand...well that's

PAWSOME!

You protect your cat through thick and thin from everything scary in the world...

I t's no exaggeration to say that—were it necessary to do so—you would take a bullet for your cat.

Fortunately, everyday life rarely presents situations of such dramatic intensity. Most of what you'll be "protecting" your cat from will be garden variety—the startling loudness of a car backfiring outside; the shifty-looking dog whose human walks him by your window every morning; the *Mad Men* opening-credits sequence, which some cats find inexplicably terrifying. (My Clayton runs in abject terror when the "falling man" makes his first appearance, and it takes him a good ten minutes to recover his equanimity).

Whether it's a veterinarian's needle or a friend's ill-behaved child or an actual lunatic shooter, there's nothing in this world so fierce, frightening, or downright petrifying that you wouldn't stand between *it* and your cat.

You may not be one of those people who can bench press their own body weight. Nevertheless, when it comes to defending your cat, you're strong and immovable as the Great Wall of China. **PAWSOME!**

...But you still make your cat feel like a fierce, brave hunter!

[To be read in an only slightly patronizing baby voice:]
Who's mommy's brave little hunter? Yes you are! YES YOU ARE!
PAWSOME!

You give your cats their favorite human foods

S haring a meal with others is one of the oldest and most important rituals of communal bonding in human history.

The same is true of human-*feline* history.

Anthropologists say that cats first started hanging around humans once we began farming, because of the plentiful rodents our storehouses of food would regularly attract. Seeing how my cats react whenever I unwrap a package of deli cheese, however, I'm guessing that the food itself was also a pretty big draw.

Fast-forward a few millennia to your own present-day household, and ask yourself what your cat would do without you and your ability to open cans of tuna, dismantle a turkey sandwich, or pull bits of cooked chicken from the bone—and then distribute this bounty to your waiting (and famished) feline friend?

My cats have assured me in no uncertain terms that they would starve—*starve*, I tell you!—if not for the near-constant stream of morsels from my own plate, bowl, or to-go container directed their way.

Chances are your cats have made you similar assurances of encroaching famine, and the necessity of fending it off with samples of your own meals.

And, also, you probably just have a lot of fun spoiling your kitties rotten.

PAWSOME!

You turn on the bathroom faucet so your cat can play in the water

I once spent seventy-five dollars on a Hammacher Schlemmer cat fountain because one of my cats was so very, very enraptured by running water—whether it came out of the kitchen sink or the bathtub faucet—that I figured I'd make us both happy (her directly, me vicariously) by giving her the gift of constant running water, whenever she wanted it.

Stop me if you already know where this story is going.

I guess they wouldn't make cat fountains if there weren't cats out there who actually liked them. Sadly for me, however, not one of my five ever has—not even the ones who were really into running water and more or less demanded it of me, repeatedly, throughout the course of the day.

Science will tell you that cats find running water to be more "natural" and hygienic, which is why they're so fascinated by it. And while that may very well be true, I have no doubt that the fun of getting their human to jump up so obligingly whenever a little bathtub playtime is requested is a big part of the attraction (for *my* cats, anyway).

Vexing as it often was to have a cat demanding I turn on the faucet for her while I was in the middle of trying to finish a tricky paragraph ahead of a writing deadline, or struggling into a too-tight pair of jeans, or getting comfortable on the couch with my husband, I suppose I can understand why the appeal of running water might lessen when it suddenly becomes available *all the time*. Scarcity is the secret sauce that adds flavor to so many of the things we love most, like the holiday meals that only come once a year, or the appearance of the ice cream truck that only cruises your block once or twice a week.

And while I didn't necessarily love having to stop whatever I was doing whenever the whim struck my faucet-loving cat, her insistence that it be the faucet—and not something she could access herself whenever she wanted—made me appreciate those scarce and fleeting pleasures in my own life that much more.

PAWSOME!

You brush your cat's teeth

I've been a cat guardian for more than twenty-five years now—and, for the past decade or so, a very public one who spends the majority of her days engaging with other cat-parents online and in person—so I thought I'd heard pretty much everything on the subject of cat care.

You can imagine my shock, therefore, when I read an article in the *Atlantic* a couple of months ago about people who brush their cats' teeth at home.

Let me say that again: There are people out there who take a toothbrush and toothpaste, load a squirt of said toothpaste onto the toothbrush, force brush and paste into their unwilling cats' clenched mouths, and *brush their cats' teeth for them.*

(!!!)

Not only is home-cat-tooth-brushing apparently a bona fide *thing*, by the way, but it's a thing that a small subset of intrepid cat guardians do *several times a week!*

Did you know about this?!!?

I'm going to guess that the vast majority of cat custodians do *not* brush their cats' teeth at home on the regular (although I do dispense a daily dose of Dental Greenies, for whatever that's worth)—and I'm going to guess further that *you*, dear reader, probably don't either.

But even if you, like me, sensibly leave your cats' dental care to trained professionals, you've undoubtedly done all kinds of other invasive and unpleasant things—things that your cats hated at the time, and possibly hated you for doing—for the sake of safeguarding their health and wellbeing. If the phrase "kitty burrito" (a method of wrapping a cat in a towel or blanket so as to trim her claws, force pills down her throat, inject a needle into the back of her neck, et cetera) strikes a resonant chord with you, then you know what I'm talking about.

Cats are indisputably adorable, and they fill our hearts and our homes with joy, laughter, and considerable entertainment. But living with a cat isn't *all* sunshine and roses. No matter how good the good times are, eventually things will get real—and you'll find yourself filling the role of live-in nurse, dealing with the up-close-and-personal realities of a fragile and aging feline body that you're responsible for keeping alive and healthy for as long as that's possible.

It's a tough job, and it's an often thankless one. (Your cat certainly isn't going to thank you!) There's no national "Cat Parents' Day." Hallmark doesn't make a card that says, *Thanks for taking such great care of your cats!* Nobody will ever hand you a trophy for doing it, or give you the key to the city, or throw you a parade.

But you weren't doing it for any of those things, anyway.

PAWSOME!

You take care of your cat when she's sick

It's a given that no home can be truly happy if there aren't any cats in it. But that doesn't mean living with a cat is all sunshine and roses.

Just like the rest of us, cats get sick sometimes. Even the healthiest kitty is apt to come down with the occasional cold or tummy bug, or twist her leg while jumping from a high-up shelf. And should you be lucky enough to avoid all the minor scrapes and skirmishes, the inevitability of old age—with its attendant illnesses and indignities—is still awaiting your cat down the road.

Like most longtime cat guardians, I've found myself having to treat wounds, change bandages, gently wash the fur of a kitty so ill that she got sick all over herself, administer pills and shots, and occasionally force-feed a cat with baby food and water mixed in a syringe. (A cat with a head cold who can't smell her food is apt to refuse to eat it, which is not at all the same thing as saying that a cat with a head cold *doesn't need* to eat.)

That my cats greeted these efforts on my part—however tenderly offered—with extreme resistance will come as a surprise to exactly no one.

You would think that after years and years of providing non-stop food and toys and cuddles, I'd have earned the teensiest bit of credibility when, for example, it comes time to give one of my cats a dose of a liquid antibiotic. Alas, you would be *very* wrong.

And so I've become an expert in the "kitty burrito" method of immobilizing my cats by wrapping them up in a towel with just their head exposed—holding the struggling, wrapped-up cat to my chest with one hand while the other attempts to get the medication into her reluctant mouth and down her throat.

(One time, one of my cat's back legs wriggled free of the "kitty burrito" and left a colorful trail of welts down the front of my chest and across my upper left arm. And that's how I learned that trying to medicate a cat while wearing a scoop-necked tank top is a strictly amateur move.)

I suppose if you were a certain kind of fair-weather friend, you'd enjoy the good times when they come—all the purrs and snuggles and delightful games of "chase the toy mouse"—while leaving your felines to fend for themselves when those good times turn decidedly less fun.

But you made a commitment to your cat the day you brought him into your life—a commitment to stand by his side and take care of him in sickness and health, no matter what. You did so knowing that love isn't always pretty and can sometimes be downright unpleasant.

But you also knew that taking the good with the bad is precisely what real love is all about.

Besides, you were never the type to bail when the going gets tough, anyway.

PAWSOME!

You take your cat to the vet, even though you both hate it

M y cat Clayton is kind of a rock star at the vet's office.

At least, you'd *think* he was a rock star based on the wildly enthusiastic greeting he receives whenever we walk in. Cries of "It's *CLAYTON!!!*" ring out from Reception in the front all the way to exam rooms in the back, as every single person we pass shoves a couple of fingers or even their whole hand through the top of Clayton's soft carrier—while Clayton himself, receiving all this adulation as no more than his fair due, purrs contentedly.

The secret of Clayton's popularity at the vet's office is really no secret at all: Clayton is one of those extraordinarily rare oddball kitties who actually likes the vet's office!

I *know!* But it's *true!*

To say that Clayton loves attention would be like saying the rest of us love oxygen. Being so utterly dependent on constant attention to get him through his days, he's not particularly partial as to where or how he gets it—not even when that attention is accompanied by intrusive fingers in his mouth, or needles in his rump, or the decidedly uncomfortable insertion of a thermometer in his backside.

The otherwise-beleaguered doctors and technicians at our vet's office are more used to cats like...well...like every other cat I've ever lived with. Cats who, upon seeing their carrier suddenly appear in the living room, will run, hide, scratch, hiss, scale impossibly tall cabinets, transform themselves into un-catchable streaks of speeding fur, and otherwise make the run-up to their vet visit among the more miserable half-hours you'll ever spend.

If you're lucky, that's the worst of it—and your cat will settle down into some more-or-less sulky form of passive resistance once you make it to the vet's office.

But every so often you have a special cat, like my Homer was. The bar-none greatest boy in the world at home, Homer was an ungodly holy terror in any medical setting. Eventually, our vet suggested in the nicest possible language that Homer probably shouldn't return to their clinic ever again—and, after assuring her that I would assume financial responsibility for any medical bills incurred by her staff as a result of Homer's visit, I was forced to concede the point.

In short: With the lovely exception of Clayton, taking my cats to the vet has been just about the most consistently harrowing thing about being a cat-mom.

My guess is that it's the same for you—that no matter how genuinely lovely and genial a person your veterinarian is, there's a small part of you that dreads any excursion to the vet's office, whether it's due to a major illness or a routine exam.

And imagine how your cat feels! Your poor kitty has no idea why you've dragged her from her safe and sunny kitty bed out into a cold cruel veterinary exam room where, in league with various medical personnel, you've inexplicably transformed from Loving Source Of Food And Comfort into Co-Conspirator With Pure Evil.

I suspect, however, that somewhere deep down, your cat knows that even this outrage—like just about everything else you do—reflects how very deep your love for her runs. That even though seeing how utterly miserable she is makes you more miserable than words could ever express, you'd suffer this and worse a thousand times over, if it means making sure your beloved feline companion stays healthy and happy for years and years to come.

PAWSOME!

You touch your nose to your cat's nose

Humans greet other humans with handshakes. Cats greet other cats—especially cats they already know—by touching noses. And while the minor exchange of scents that occurs between cats when they touch noses isn't really *your* thing, you understand how much this friendly little gesture means to your kitty.

So you touch your nose to her nose. And she touches her nose to yours. And the whole thing is soooooooooooo sweet that it's more than just adorable.

It's **PAWSOME!**

You debase yourself for your cats' amusement

My husband used to think I was sharp as a tack. My keen intellect was one of the things that first drew him to me, he always said. That and a general air of cosmopolitan sophistication.

Then I moved into his apartment with my three cats. It was no more than a day or two into our cohabitation when my husband (then-boyfriend) heard me, in a goofy falsetto, query of my cat Homer, "Was dose nom-noms so nummy? Was dey so nummy in yo wizzle tummy?"

It's probably not an exaggeration to say that, in the eighteen years since, his opinion of my intellect hasn't entirely recovered.

What can I say? A fear of looking foolish isn't really one of my biggest fears. It comes well behind, for example, a fear of finding hairs on my chin (this has happened three times since I turned fifty), or a spider in my bed, or pretty much anything that would require me to spend some significant amount of time in any kind of natural setting that wasn't a beach.

And while I'd generally prefer *not* to look foolish in front of others, the things that tickle my cats' fancy tend to take precedence. Besides, as I've painstakingly explained to my husband more times than I can count, if I *don't* speak to my cats in that voice, how will they know I'm talking to them and not somebody else?

Who among us hasn't found themselves wriggling around on their belly so as to be at cat's-eye level when playing a game of Swipe

The Toy Mouse In My Hand? Or babbling incoherently in their special talking-to-my-cat voice?

And, sure, I sometimes find myself intimidated by those frighteningly put-together women I see on TV or roaming the streets of Manhattan. Women in four-figure suits with the kind of straight shiny hair that *somebody* obviously spent hours blowing out for them, and who look as if phrases like *nom noms* and *fuzzy wuzzy* would never in a million years cross their immaculately made-up lips.

But then I reflect that those women have probably never known the joys of donning a plastic hula skirt still hanging around your closet from some decades-old Halloween party, and swishing it around like a person in the throes of some sort of fit, just for the sheer fun of watching your cat chase after you while swiping furiously at the fringe.

PAWSOME!

You build your schedule around your cat's schedule

Dog owners are forever being valorized for their high-intensity commitment to their furry pals—blowing off after-work outings so they can rush home and walk their dogs; taking their dogs for walks even during typhoons and blizzards; and devoting hours and hours to hanging out at dog parks solely for their dogs' benefit.

This very public sacrifice of scarce personal time at the altar of dog worship is one reason, I think, why dog owners are perceived as being more "social" and "well adjusted" than cat people—not only because all that time spent watching dogs socialize at dog parks seems to imply lots of human interaction, as well (although mostly what I see at the dog park is people sitting on benches and checking their cell phones, while pointedly ignoring their fellow dog owners), but also because the conspicuous sacrifice of one's precious time for the sake of the greater good is the very glue that holds society together.

Antisocial cat people, on the other hand (or so the general perception goes), have cats instead of dogs because they selfishly wanted a companion animal who wouldn't impose on their free time.

The thing with cats and their guardians is that cats spend the majority of their time indoors, far from public view. There's nothing even a little bit performative about all that time you spend doing things with and for your cats, because nobody's ever around to see any of it. Even in the case of the cats whose humans walk them outdoors on leashes, they're not taking those cats to "cat parks" or following them around with little poop bags, or leaving them tied to a nearby chair at some outdoor café while their human enjoys brunch with friends.

It's this very lack of visibility that makes it seem as though dog owners are endlessly self-sacrificing, while cat owners...not so much.

What almost nobody outside your innermost circle is ever likely to see is how much of your schedule is built around your cat's schedule. Cats are creatures of habit, after all, and, to the greatest extent possible, cats like doing the same things at the exact same times every day.

Which is why you get up early even on your days off to feed your cat at the time he's used to. It's why you let your cat, who's accustomed to being in bed with you from precisely 11:00 p.m. until 7:00 a.m. every night, sprawl all over you even when a bout of insomnia would probably pass more quickly if you had the bed to yourself. It's why you're infinitely more discerning about whom you allow into the inner sanctum of your life and your home—the one and only place in the whole world where your cat feels entirely comfortable and secure—than the caretakers of an easygoing dog are required to be.

Cat guardians don't get as much glory for their constancy because it tends to manifest itself in that same place where our innermost hearts always live: within the privacy of our very own homes.

PAWSOME!

Sometimes you break down and smell your cat's butt

I mean, it would be kinda hard *not* to, given how frequently it seems to end up pressed right against your face...

At least your cat keeps it pretty clean, right???

PAWSOME!

You always give your cat a lap to sit on

Everybody remembers *The Giving Tree*, Shel Silverstein's parable about a selfless apple tree who loved a little boy and gave him all of herself—her apples for him to eat, her branches for him to climb (and later to build a house with), her leaves to shade his head, and her trunk for him to carve into a boat. Eventually the tree was nothing more than a stump—but still she had one final thing to offer up: a place for the boy, now an elderly man, to sit and rest.

To my fellow selfless cat lovers out there, I say: We are all that Giving Tree.

Of course, not every cat actually wants to sit on us or snuggle into our laps. For sixteen years, I had the exclusive love of a "surly girl" named Scarlett, who never craved much in the way of physical affection beyond a desire to sprawl behind me on the back of the couch and rest a single paw on my shoulder while she slept. My cat Homer, on the other hand, demanded *lots* of physical contact—although what he primarily wanted was to lean against my leg rather than lie on it. My cat Vashti eschewed laps and legs entirely in favor of lying on the chests of the humans she especially liked.

These days I'm owned by two true-blue lap cats, and rare are the times when neither my husband nor I have a cat sprawled across our legs. In fact, just finding a handful of lap-cat-free moments over the course of the day—to use the restroom, perhaps, or to engage in a bit of husband/wife alone time—can be a job of work, one inevitably accompanied by a series of bitterly drawn-out feline complaints that could only be translated as: *But whyyyyyyyyyyyyyyyyyyyyy?!?!?*

The point, however, isn't whether your cat sleeps on your literal lap. The point is that, dollars to donuts, whatever it is your cat wants from you, you offer it up gladly—even if what you have to offer is nothing more than a warm place for her to lay her weary kitty head.

The Giving Tree's got nothing on you.

PAWSOME!

You fish your cat's toys out from under the couch and refrigerator

E very so often, I'll notice that the floors of my home—normally covered in a thin layer of crinkle balls, rattling felt mice, catnip sachets, and wadded up takeout receipts—seem suspiciously clean. I'll make it all the way from the staircase through the living room and into the kitchen without having to sidestep so much as a single plastic spring. *That's odd,* I'll think. *I haven't done any housecleaning since [INSERT DATE AT LEAST TWO MONTHS PREVIOUS].*

While I loathe dirt and generally try to stay on top of the dust situation due to allergies, I'm not exactly a neat freak—and I've been more than happy over the years to relinquish the floors of my home to the cats. They, in turn, have converted our throw rugs into scratch pads, our standing knick-knacks into...well...into more scratch pads, and our floorboards and tiles themselves into a kind of ad-hoc toybox.

So when I encounter a tidy floor—knowing, as I do, that it certainly has nothing to do with my own endeavors—it can mean only one thing: All the cat toys in the house have migrated to one of two Toy Graveyards.

I refer, of course, to the space under the sofa and the crevice beneath the refrigerator.

The rule that any and all cat toys will eventually end up under some large piece of furniture —including items that are only incidentally "cat toys," like used tin-foil balls or yarn-tasseled bookmarks—is as immutable as Newton's laws of motion. Given the endless batting-around of said toys that the typical cat engages in, simple physics demands that, eventually, an overly enthusiastic swipe will direct the item in question to the irresistible gravitational pull of the black hole under the couch or below the fridge.

Some of this is deliberate, cats being pretty much addicted to hiding things and then "finding" them a few seconds or even a few days later. In our house, hiding a small plastic mouse beneath the living-room area rug on Tuesday, where it can be rediscovered on Friday, is a little gift that Past Clayton likes to leave for Future Clayton—or, occasionally, for Present Mom, who's apt to stumble witlessly into the sharp corner of an end table upon accidentally tripping over the unexpected lump in the rug.

The only trouble, of course, is that even the best-laid plans of mice and men (and cats) are apt to go awry. Inevitably, your cat will be so successful at "hiding" some favored toy—or so *un*successful at keeping it in play—that it will be up to you to lie flat down on your belly with your cheek welded to the floor, clutching a broom or unbent coat hanger or maybe even an actual fishing pole, while you grope around in the hopes of unearthing Mopsy's and Mittens' favorite playthings.

It's a dirty job—especially in my house, where chances are nobody's swept under the sofa or refrigerator since the *last* time we had to fish out all the cat toys—but it's one you do without complaining, simply because you're an amazing human who loves your cat.

PAWSOME!

You change the channel when there's something scary on TV

P erhaps you live with what I'll call a "noise-sensitive" cat.

Maybe you've gotten used to opening new trash bags veeeeeeeeerrrrry slooooooooooooowly rather than with a decisive *snap!* Maybe you take your shoes off the moment you enter the house—not for the sake of hygiene, but because the sound of heels clicking briskly across hardwood floors leaves your cat convinced the Apocalypse has arrived. Maybe every time you open a stepladder with a loud *CLANG!* is a newly traumatic event for your cat, one that requires you to stop whatever you're doing and comfort him before you can resume the task at hand.

If this describes you and your cat, chances are you gave up watching jump-scare movies in your house a long time ago. The same holds true for movies with lots of loud shooting sequences, including just about anything in the explosive Marvel or *Star Wars* canons. My husband and I have even learned to hit the "skip intro" button ASAP when watching old *Mad Men* reruns, because something about the combination of the opening-credits music and the silhouetted "falling man" scares our poor Clayton nearly out of his wits.

That last example just goes to prove that you can never be entirely sure ahead of time what's going to set a sensitive kitty off. Sometimes the most innocuous thing onscreen will send a startled Bootsie skittering for cover, while you're left to suss out what it was, exactly, about the bucolic British countryside in that episode of *Father Brown Murder Mysteries* that scared the bejesus out of your poor puss.

Not that it really matters—because, in the end, you do what needs to be done: You put your own viewing pleasure on pause, decide to wait until you're alone later on to find out whodunit, and open up that peaceful "TV For Cats" streaming app you downloaded onto your Fire Cube for just such an occasion.

Seriously, though...*whodunit???*

PAWSOME!

You don't get offended when your cat starts vigorously cleaning himself the second you stop petting him

A s with so many mysterious feline behaviors, the question, "Why does my cat vigorously groom himself the second I stop petting him?" has any number of theoretical answers.

It might be because your cat is itchy or sensitive in that one spot you were just petting. Or perhaps because he's replicating the kind of grooming behavior he would have experienced with his biological mom (i.e. where she teaches her kittens to groom by grooming them with her tongue and then having them groom themselves). Sometimes it may be indicative of an underlying problem, like chronically dry skin or an over-sensitivity to touch known as hyperesthesia syndrome, which can make petting an uncomfortable or even painful experience for your kitty.

But, in most cases, the answer's a pretty simple one: Cats just like grooming themselves.

Like, they really, *really* like grooming themselves—so much so that anywhere from 30% to 50% of their waking hours are spent on grooming. (A statistic that would have impressed even the vainest of my college sorority sisters.)

Cats are also pretty fastidious when it comes to things like cleanliness and odor, and no matter how much your cat might enjoy smelling your scent (you *are* her favorite person, after all!), she doesn't necessarily want to smell you all over herself.

This distinction sounds reasonable enough, but it can still feel kind of...well...maybe a little insulting when your cat deploys her raspy tongue to the patch of fur you were just petting, and cleans with the kind of intensity you probably wouldn't exhibit in your own personal grooming unless you'd just taken an accidental tumble into a septic tank.

You might even find yourself inclined to sniff under your arms and wonder aloud—à la Duckie in *Pretty in Pink*—"Do I *offend*?"

But it's hard to feel *too* offended when every moment your cat spends grooming is an opportunity for you to appreciate the adorable perfection of her pink and oh-so-raspy tongue.

PAWSOME!

You leave your cat alone when she wants to be left alone...

The way in which all cats and Greta Garbo are alike is in their frequent desire to be left *ahlone*.

Not that your cat doesn't love hanging out with you. You're her very favorite person in the whole entire world. But, still...sometimes the prospect of chilling in an empty room, gazing out of a window with nothing but your thoughts and a few wispy, trailing daydreams for company, sounds like an irresistible prospect.

There's a certain kind of person—let's call them "dog owners"—who wouldn't be able to help but take it personally if their beloved four-legged companion were to indicate a desire for a bit of solo, no-humans-allowed time.

But cat guardians are infinitely wiser. Much like our cats, we understand that a little time set aside for mental rejuvenation only makes us more attentive spouses, parents, friends, and coworkers.

And, even aside from that, solitude just feels nice sometimes. Which is why we would never want to deny that same simple pleasure to our cats.

PAWSOME!

...But you give your cat lots of attention when she wants it!

I can be walking up the stairs in my house, balancing a stack of clean laundry that goes up to my chin while simultaneously talking to my mom on the phone that's pressed between my shoulder and my ear—but if one of my cats paws at my leg, I tell mom to hold on, shuffle the laundry so it's now teetering on only one arm, and somehow manage to kneel down without pitching headlong down the staircase to find out what, exactly, my cat wants of me.

Nine times out of ten, the attention itself is what he wants.

Logically I know that there any number of things more important—or, at minimum, more immediately urgent—than whether or not one of my cats wants a scritch or a treat or even just momentary eye contact *right this second*. Cookies left in the oven even a minute too long are apt to flatten into hockey pucks. Amazon is seconds away from selling out of the $30, size 7 ½ walking shoes I love because they really do feel like walking on a cloud (which is why they sell out almost instantly). Balancing all that laundry *plus* the phone *while I'm walking up a staircase* actually requires whatever attention I can spare so as to keep from falling backwards to my death.

Between the word "death" above and this very sentence, by the way, lies an unseen 10-minute gap in my writing, during which I hoisted my three-legged Clayton onto my lap, helped him arrange himself so as to have the best view through the windows next to my desk and out to the backyard—and, of course, entirely forgot how I was going to end that last paragraph.

(I live with the persistent yet ultimately unprovable belief that an entire coherent novel could be constructed out of all the forgotten ideas, sentences, and half-grafs that will forever remain unwritten, because I stopped what I was doing to pay attention to a relentless cat.)

Magazine articles and self-help gurus are fond of telling us that we all rush around too much, that we let concerns about work and money dominate our thoughts, that we don't spend enough time being "present" when we're with our loved ones, or in our lives in general.

Maybe that's true. Still, I'm willing to bet cash money that nothing and no one is so important that it/they can't be postponed for just a minute or two, so that you can spend some mindful moments—right here, right now—giving your beloved feline all the attention she endlessly craves and oh-so-richly deserves.

PAWSOME!

You give your cat chin scritches

A nd they feel soooooooooooo gooooooooood...

PAWSOME!

You give your cat some tuna whenever you open a can

Maybe you've been on the receiving end of a lecture from your veterinarian about why you shouldn't feed your cats tuna. For starters, even a small portion is too high in calories for the typical cat. Eating too much of it can lead to obesity, along with all of obesity's concomitant complications (diabetes, UTIs, high blood pressure, et cetera).

And tuna is far from nutritionally balanced. It has too much unsaturated fat and not enough Vitamin E or any of the other antioxidants your kitty needs to stay healthy. Not to mention that tuna's high in mercury, and eating too much of it can lead to mercury poisoning.

But—with the exception of the mercury thing—couldn't the same be said about nearly any of the fun foods that *you* like to treat yourself to once in a while? Could you really make a compelling argument to your doctor along the lines of, "You don't understand, Doc. I actually *need* to consume loaded potato skins and chocolate cheesecake on a regular basis for...um...health reasons."

By the same token, would you want to live a life utterly devoid of loaded potato skins or chocolate cheesecake?

Of course you wouldn't! And neither would your cat—for whom that giant spoonful of tuna is basically his chocolate cheesecake equivalent.

It's one thing if your veterinarian has told you there's some specific reason why your cat should never have tuna. But assuming your cat is reasonably healthy, and the dispensing of tuna is an occasional treat, then why shouldn't little Simba have some every now and then, when he clearly loves it sooooooooooooooooooo much?

And isn't half the fun of opening that can of tuna for your own lunch seeing how utterly gaga your kitty gets upon hearing the whir of the can opener, knowing that in mere moments he'll be enjoying a sweet spoonful of the good stuff—dispensed by you, the amazing creature who makes all his days so fun-filled and satisfying?

PAWSOME!

You incorporate cat stuff into your decor

T here are any number of feline-inspired items for the dedicated ailurophile to work into their décor if the mood strikes: cat-decorated sheets, blankets, bowls, towels, and throw pillows; cat-shaped wall clocks, lamps, bookends, and footstools; tissue dispensers and coasters that look like a cat's wazoo.

But that's not what I'm talking about here.

When I say you incorporate "cat stuff" into your décor, I mean those empty shelves on the living room wall that might look as if they're there to hold various knickknacks and bric-a-brac, but that are actually there because your cat enjoys having a high vantage point from which to survey the living room.

Or the shoe boxes that haven't held a pair of shoes for at least six months, but that do hold a fuzzy cat body for at least one hour every day.

Or that blanket still folded across the back of your couch—even though it's summer and ninety-five degrees outside, and the mere thought of a blanket makes the backs of your knees start to sweat—because no matter how hot it is outside, your cat *loooooooooooves* how very warm and soft sleeping on that blanket is.

And then there's the legit cat furniture scattered about your home—climbers and scratchers and various plush beds—just because they make your kitty happy.

A visiting stranger might think you're decidedly on the "eccentric" side upon taking all this in for the first time. But who cares what judgmental strangers think? After all, the good opinion of people you barely know means infinitely less than building a home that makes it clear your cat is an essential, and much-beloved, member of your family.

PAWSOME!

You know that how you spend on your cat is more important than what you spend

E very so often, I'll see a YouTube video or online photo series about some absolute Xanadu of a cat home—a house replete with cat-sized tunnels and colorful shelves and elevated walkways all along the walls and ceilings. Maybe there's even an elaborate two-story "catio,"which is a screened-in outdoor area where an indoor cat can feel like he's interacting with nature—or, at least, as much of nature as one can find in the backyards of the suburban homes where such catios are inevitably built.

But there I go, sounding kind of snide about it—when the truth is I'm so consumed with envy, I can barely see straight.

Of course I'd love to turn my home into a star-spangled maze of tactile delights for my cats. Of course there's literally nothing I see—online or IRL—that I think *might* make my cats happy without simultaneously thinking, *Should I buy this for my cats right now?* And while the dream of a catio is one that, for various logistical reasons (mainly involving the unwieldy architecture of my very old house), likely won't come to fruition anytime soon, that doesn't stop me from breaking my heart over the lack of such a luxury in my highly indulged cats' lives.

The biggest obstacle, needless to say, is money. I only have so much of it, and the lion's share is dedicated to the same wearying list of drudgeries that everyone else's is: food, shelter, health care, and responsible savings against old age and/or a possible rainy day.

And yet, I think my two cats are just about as happy as any two cats could be. I may not be able to decorate my whole house for them, but I invested in a sturdy cat tree nearly a decade ago that still looks and stands just fine, and installed it in the sunniest corner of my home where my sun-worshipping cat, Fanny, can ascend to its highest tower and bask in sunlight all year round. My other cat, Clayton, is highly partial to crinkle balls and those little plastic toy mice with feathered tails that make a rattling sound when you shake them—a toy that costs all of about $0.99, and of which he therefore gets one or two new specimens every week.

But my cats' *real* favorite thing (aside from catnip, which I buy in a big econo-size jug once a year and distribute with a free hand) is lap-time with mom. Fanny likes to get a vigorous round of lap-based back scratching every morning, whereas Clayton insists on long, sprawling naps across my legs in the afternoons.

I'm pleased to be able to offer both in essentially unlimited quantities.

It's easy to feel that competitive spark upon seeing someone whose kids—whether those kids have four legs or two—seem to have toys and baubles and all kinds of advantages that yours simply don't and never could on your own earth-based salary.

But your fur-kids still have the single greatest advantage any fur-kid could ever have:

You for their cat-parent.

PAWSOME!

You let your cat sleep in bed with you

I've read all the so-called "experts" who say it's a bad idea to let your cats sleep in bed with you, and all I can say about that is, *phooey!*

Phooey! I say.

Living with cats and *not* letting them sleep in bed with you is about as much fun as going to the beach in a wool suit. It's about as much fun as attending school on a Saturday. It's about as much fun as taking all the singing and dancing out of *The Lion King* and turning it back into *Hamlet*.

Not that there aren't a *very* few downsides. There's waking up eyeball to...um...eyeball with the business end of a kitty tush, for example. Or sometimes finding yourself crowded off your own pillows because that's where little Trixie likes to stretch out. You may occasionally have less freedom to move your legs if your cats are snoozing at the foot of your bed. Too much jostling is likely to disturb their slumber—and lord knows it would be downright cruel to rob your moggy of even one minute out of the 960 minutes or so she spends napping each and every day.

But you'd have to be a true curmudgeon to resent any of that when it so clearly makes your cat very, *very* happy snuggle up close to you at night. She loves your warmth, your familiar smell, and the cozy feeling of being *purr*fectly protected when sleeping beside you, the only human in the whole wide world in whom she has complete and absolute trust.

As for what *you* get out of it…well…what sane person could deny that the sound of purring as you drift off to sleep is absolutely, one hundred percent

PAWSOME!

You cuddle with your cat on sick days

Y ears of research has consistently shown that cuddling up close to your resident feline can lower blood pressure and relieve symptoms of anxiety and depression. There's evidence that cats' purrs help broken bones mend more swiftly. Best of all, cuddle-time with cats can speed up recovery from most major and minor illnesses, including the trifling colds and flus that probably account for the majority of sick days you end up taking.

That's how cuddling with your cats on sick days benefits *you*.

From your cat's *purr*spective, your sick days are probably some of the best days around. Chances are he can't think of a single better way to pass the time than snuggling up close to you under the covers while you watch TV or read a book, or simply bask in the unaccustomed luxury of a loooooong afternoon snooze. (This is a luxury with which your cat is *highly* familiar!)

The tragedy of it (as far as your cat's concerned) is that days where you can actually remain abed for hours on end, just like your pampered puss does, probably don't come more than once or twice in a year.

But when they do come, these are great good days, indeed. Which is why the selflessness of your taking the time to make your cat soooooo happy—even in the midst of your own chest cold or sore back, or whatever else it is that's keeping you trapped in bed—is nothing short of **PAWSOME!**

You let your cat snuggle between you and the arm of the chair

When it comes to comfy napping spots, probably nothing will ever be better for your cat than the coziness of a cardboard box or paper shopping bag that's just the right size—large enough to squeeze his whole body into, but small enough to feel snug and secure on all sides.

A pretty close second, though, is when your cat is able to wedge his entire body between yours and the arm of the sofa or recliner or plain old office chair you happen to be sitting in.

The warmth of it! The comforting, familiar smell of his favorite human! The feeling of being one-hundred percent safe from any and all predators who might very well be stalking your quiet, suburban neighborhood *at this very moment!*

Granted, it's not always entirely comfortable for *you*. Having a cat's body wedged between you and the arm of the couch might make it difficult to curl up in your preferred lounging position, or to use that sofa arm to prop up the book you're reading.

But how much does any of that matter? A teensy bit of discomfort is such a small price to pay, after all, for something that makes your kitty feel so very, very good.

PAWSOME!

You let your cat sleep in your favorite spot

I never really liked to share when I was a kid—not pizza or paint brushes or favorite toys.

This was especially true when it came to my personal space. As a bookish kid, I had specific little nooks and corners where I liked to curl up to read, and woe betide the playful sibling or well-meaning adult who tried to insert themselves into that space.

I was kind of selfish, is what I'm trying to say—and may well have grown from a selfish childhood into a selfish young adulthood, followed by a selfish middle age, if not for the timely intercession of the cats I first adopted in my early twenties.

I can't exactly say that my cats taught me generosity by their own big-hearted example, because cats are as territorial as any creature on the face of the earth.

It's more like they conditioned me over time, until sharing became an automatic process. Now, not only do I sit or lie someplace else—without even thinking twice!—when I happen to walk into a room and see one of my cats snoozing away in my own favorite spot, but I also smile affectionately at the sight of it.

If Childhood Me could see Adult Me, she'd be amazed at how far I've come.

PAWSOME!

You play "cat soccer" with crumpled balls of paper

M aybe you've never been much of a jock.

Maybe your participation in high school athletics is better described as "reluctant" than "record-breaking." Maybe you've had a pair of running shoes sitting next to your front door since New Year's Eve *last* year, which was when you promised yourself you'd pick up a jogging regimen that still hasn't quite materialized.

Okay, so you're not a gym rat. But that doesn't mean you can't engage with your cat in a spirited game of "cat soccer" (toss paper ball to cat, watch as cat bats paper ball around, repeat), or "throw and retrieve the plastic mouse" (knowing full well that you'll do both the throwing and the retrieving in this particular game).

Maybe your high school coach never saw you as anything more than bench-warming material. As far as your besotted kitty's concerned, however, you're first-string all the way!

PAWSOME!

You turn your floor into a minefield of garbage...er, "toys"

I used to watch that A&E show *Hoarders* with the morbid fascination of a person recognizing scenes from her own potential future.

Not that I'm a hoarder, or even much of a saver. If anything, I probably go too far in the other direction, being just as apt to discard an outdated but still wearable pair of shoes, or old boyfriends' mix tapes (who even *has* a cassette player anymore?) as I am things that are genuinely old, broken, or useless.

Nevertheless, the floors of just about every room of my house are strewn with...well...let's just call things what they are and say *garbage*. Garbage that no living soul—save for the two thoroughly spoiled feline companions who share my home—would understand the use or necessity of. Garbage that, in darker moments, I imagine some kindly intentioned cadre of professional organizers carting remorselessly away, while I stand on the sidelines wringing my hands and piteously wailing, "But I *NEED* all this stuff!"

My living room alone is a veritable minefield of straws, bottle caps, cardboard toilet-paper rolls, wads of discarded writing paper (discarded paper always being in abundant supply in a writer's house), and crumpled-up receipts that probably first entered the house in one of the many, *many* paper bags that have also taken up semi-permanent residence. And, of course, the good folks at

Amazon keep us in enough variously sized cardboard boxes to outfit an army of cats.

If you're a cat lover, then chances are you have a similar story to tell about shoeboxes and ping-pong balls that linger on the floors of your home despite having long outlived their actual usefulness. And there they'll remain—creating clutter and collecting dust—even if your own aesthetic runs toward the sleek and minimalist, for no other reason than the fact that your kitties enjoy them.

Because that's just the kind of thoughtful person you are.

PAWSOME!

You turn the heater up way too high because your cat likes it toasty

C ats have managed to make their way into just about every corner of this world occupied by humans, no matter how icy or desolate some of those locales may be. Yet all cats—including snow-ready breeds like Maine Coons and Norwegian Forest cats—are descended from desert-dwelling African wild cats. And while heat is pretty much the defining characteristic of a desert, they also tend to be dangerously cold places at night.

This is all by way of explaining why, to this day, a cat's natural instinct is to soak up as much heat as possible while heat's available—the better to stockpile it against potential life-threatening night chills. This is true even if you and your cat live close to the Equator and enjoy balmy evenings all year round.

My own cat Fanny is as much a sun worshipper as her desert-dwelling ancestors ever were. And on those gray winter days when there's nary a ray of sunlight to be found, Fanny makes do with a heated cat bed resting directly in front of the giant, Nineteenth-century radiators our Nineteenth-century house came equipped with. And from there she stretches and flips over contentedly—heating first her belly, then her back, and then her belly again—all winter long.

Those giant radiators are pretty effective at warming up our drafty, high-ceilinged home. A bit *too* effective at times, actually. The desk where I do my writing sits right next to one of them, and I'll admit there are times when the heat gets to be too much for me.

Like, waaaaaay too much for me. And I'm a Florida native! Ten-year-old me used to run around outside in ninety-degree heat all summer long! So it's more than a little odd to find myself, all these years later, sweating my face off way up here in the frozen northeast while snow falls and ice puddles form outside.

It's not like I can't decrease the level of heat our radiators radiate. Mere steps from my desk is a fancy, computer-controlled wall panel that lets me do exactly that.

And yet, when I look over at Fanny and see how *very* happy all that heat makes her, I can't quite bring myself to do it.

I'll wager that most of us have made a similar decision at one time or another—the decision to endure a certain amount of physical discomfort just for the sake of making our cats happy. Not to mention, being a touch too warm during the winter months still beats the alternative.

PAWSOME!

You let your cat knead the roll above the waistband of your jeans

If you're at all like me, your physique has taken a few downward turns as you've aged out of your teens and twenties (and thirties, and...), which was probably when you last aspired to the long, lean torso that (let's face it) you now have no hope of attaining, short of an encounter with Aladdin's magic lamp.

And, maybe also like me, while you're not *embarrassed* by having a belly with a bit of a wobble, it's not like you're trying to draw everyone's attention to that fact, either.

One of the very best things about animals, and cats in particular, is how blissfully unselfconscious they are. Things that would turn you beet-red with mortification don't faze your cat in the slightest. Which is why, for example, your kitty has no second thoughts at all about planting herself smack in the middle of the living room rug while you have company over, hoisting her hind leg high in the air, and applying the cleansing scour of a raspy tongue to her nether regions with tremendous alacrity—and without the slightest twinge of embarrassment.

And which is also possibly why it never seems to occur to Ms. Mittens that you might have any feelings about that telltale roll of flesh around your midsection (one exacerbated to its fullest plumpness by the unforgiving denim waistband of your jeans) other than vicarious pleasure in the joy it gives her to knead and knead and *knead* away at it with her front paws.

It's probably the height of hypocrisy that we adore a mushy belly on a cat, yet tend to turn a disdainful eye at signs of similar mushiness in our fellow humans—a disdainful eye that we also, sadly, sometimes turn on ourselves.

Nevertheless, as a true-blue cat lover, you're more than willing to endure the emotional pain (and sometimes very real physical pain!) of having your cat remind you of this particular shortcoming while her happy little claws and paw pads work away at it.

And maybe you're even secretly kind of glad it's there—something of yourself you can offer to your cat now, in the full flush of your wise old(er) age, that you didn't have to offer in your twenties.

PAWSOME!

You sit near your cat, but not too near your cat

A ffectionate cuddling is all well and good, but everybody needs a little *purr*-sonal space sometimes, amirite? **PAWSOME!**

You overlook your cat's bad manners

Cats have a reputation for being aloof, circumspect, somewhat snooty creatures—all of which seem like incongruous things to go along with a charge of "bad manners." In fact, I can almost hear readers out there clutching their pearls and huffily exclaiming, *Bad manners??? My little Muffin??? How dare you?!*

But what else can you call it when someone, for example, takes to knocking glasses over on the coffee table for no apparent reason? Or cleans their hindquarters in public? Or yowls insistently while you're in the middle of talking to someone else? Last night, I even witnessed my cat Clayton gently place his paw in my husband's dinner plate—hoping to purloin a slice of turkey—when he thought nobody was looking.

Surely we can all agree that any human dinner guest who did such a thing would never make the Emily Post hall of fame.

The counterargument to this, naturally, is that things that seem rude to *us* are far less so when placed in the context of what might be termed "cat custom." Cat custom dictates, for example, that sniffing a newcomer's hindquarters is *good* manners. And it's not like your cat can say, "Pass the turkey." How else is he supposed to ask for that slice sitting on your plate?

Isn't the real offense against hospitality that you didn't offer any turkey to your cat in the first place?

But just the fact that you're thinking this way when it comes to your cats' alleged breaches of etiquette indicates an acceptance of the customs of others, and alternative ways of doing things, that speaks to a certain open-mindedness on your part—an important but nevertheless rare quality, and one that's fostered by your relationship with your cat. Live and let live, you say. What's important isn't judging the nitty-gritty specific way others choose to do things like sharing food at mealtime or greeting a returned family member when she walks in the door. It's the fact that they choose to do those things with *us* that matters.

If there were more people like you, the world would be an infinitely better place!

PAWSOME!

You let your cat climb you like a tree trunk

N ot every cat's a climber, but the ones who are *really* love to climb. They'll clamber up the drapes, claw their way up the side of the couch, and scramble to the tippy top of their cat tree, where they'll pose triumphantly atop the very highest perch. I've even seen a determined cat ascend all the way to the top of a completely vertical, seven-foot bookcase (and then have no earthly idea how to get back down).

Climbing is a behavior that's evolutionarily hardwired into cats. Felines in the wild are both predator and prey, and trees are not only handy hiding spots—the better from which to launch surprise attacks while simultaneously remaining out of reach of their own would-be attackers—they also offer enough height to allow a cat to survey the terrain for miles around.

Your kitty doesn't need to worry about such things, of course. But much like humans, who no longer need to run from lions and mammoths but who now run for fun, many indoor cats still get a kick out of scaling to the highest heights your home has to offer.

But it's not just the destination that matters. That journey to the top is fun all on its own. And what could be more fun for your frisky feline than using *you*, her beloved and devoted slave, as a human tree trunk? Why not employ your denim-clad legs as a handy shortcut to the kitchen counter? (So much more entertaining than jumping straight from the floor!) And if it's your shoulder that's the goal—some cats having a fondness for riding around on human shoulders the way Indian rajas once rode in on elephants—then climbing directly up your legs just makes sense.

Of course, the main difference between you and an actual tree trunk is that a tree's bark is significantly tougher than human flesh. Your fluffy little kitty's surprisingly sharp claws probably do a lot more damage to you than they would to a tree's rough skin.

Sometimes love is pain. That's why you take it like a champ!

PAWSOME!

You wake up early, even on your days off, to feed your cat

C hances are you think of yourself, at least occasionally, as someone who works hard to give her cat a better life.

Your cats enjoy all the playtime they want, and that's because most of *your* time is spent toiling away for a boss who's kind of a jerk, alongside coworkers who don't quite rise to the level of oddball camaraderie depicted on *The Office*. Hopefully, though, you have a couple of days off in the typical week, when you can hypothetically sleep well into the early afternoon if you feel like it. (And if you're still young enough to be able to sleep that late. Ah, the things I failed to appreciate when I was in my twenties!)

I'm an early riser, myself. Mostly I wake up early to get to work, because even we self-employed writer types have to deal with deadlines, and work-related emails, and tasks assigned by the people we answer to, and things to check over from the people who answer to us.

Even on my days off, though, I'd never dream of lying in bed more than twenty minutes (at most!) past my usual time. And that's because my cats' bellies—much like *all* cats' bellies—never take a day off. It could be six a.m. on a deadline day when I have to get pages to my editor no later than seven...or it could be six a.m. on Christmas Day, when absolutely nobody I work with wants to hear from me.

Either way, if I'm not awake and at least alert enough to trudge downstairs and dump some food into a bowl, there's going to be hell to pay. As the old adage goes, there's no snooze button on a hungry cat.

Your friends who don't have cats probably feel some combination of pity and smugness when they hear tales of your early-morning wakeups in service of your four-legged bestie. *Imagine getting up THAT early just to feed a cat!*

And, sure, they may have a point. But those poor saps will also never know the joys of waking up to the sound of purring on the pillow next to their head, to the feeling of a little pink nose booping their own, to the delightful shiver of a single velvety paw brushing against their cheek, creating that tiny moment of intense love and fulfilment before they have to face the grim realities of the day.

Most of all, they'll never know how great it feels to begin each and every day by providing complete happiness and satisfaction to another living soul—accomplished with no more difficulty than a mere flick of the wrist and a pop-top can of cat food.

PAWSOME!

You hang out with your cat, doing nothing but enjoying each other's company

T hese are some of the very best moments of your own life.

And as for how your cat feels about them?
Sheer and utter *purr*fection!
PAWSOME!

You let your cat explore the deep, dark recesses of closets, cabinets, and drawers

C ats are famously curious creatures, and curiosity all on its own would be ample justification for your kitty's longing to explore all the nooks and crannies of your closets, cabinets, and drawers—darkly mysterious treasure troves of moldering old shoe boxes or tempting morsels of spilled foods.

Chances are you have one cat in particular who's especially fond of dark corners. In our home, that cat is Fanny. I once (this is a true story) spent quite some time saving up for a ridiculously expensive and thoroughly impractical pair of boots that I nonetheless coveted with an unholy lust. Having finally procured them, I stored them in their accompanying dust bag deep in the back of my closet...only to find, when I went to put them on for the first time some two months later, that Fanny had left a series of tiny raised claw marks all over the leather upper of one of the boots.

I can only blame myself, I suppose, for not having remembered that a) Fanny likes to spend a good chunk of her daily hours buried in the closet and b) the boots' dust bag—while unfailingly protecting them from dust—was never likely to offer much protection from a set of persistent claws.

The lesson I gleaned from this incident wasn't that I should keep my cats out of the closet—rather, it was that I should keep anything I valued on a high-enough shelf that the cats wouldn't be able to reach it.

How could I keep my cats out of my closets, anyway? Or from napping atop a pricey pile of cashmere sweaters in an open drawer? I mean, I know *how*, of course—being, despite ample evidence to the contrary, bright enough to understand how a locked door or closed drawer would be capable of physically repelling a cat's attempt to get at the goodies inside.

What I mean is, how could I bring myself to do it? How could any of us?

Loving a cat means looking for ways to make them happy. Even if making them happy means occasionally letting them play Lewis and Clark in your pantry or in the back of your closet.

Even if making them happy means sometimes allowing them to spelunk in the depths of your sock drawer.

Even if making them happy means sacrificing a super-cool pair of boots that you really, really, *really* wanted.

It's all right, though. Everybody knows that people who live to make others happy are totally and completely

PAWSOME!

You spoil your cats rotten

M y husband isn't especially difficult to figure out—an attribute that I note here with a great deal of approval. Cats are hard enough to understand without throwing an excessively complicated human housemate into the mix.

Still, there are times when he manages to leave me completely befuddled. Like when he walks into the living room and finds me on the couch with a velvet cushion on my lap, atop which my cat Clayton is sprawled on his back while I give him a thorough tummy rub, and he will say (my husband, that is) with a clear note of disapproval in his voice:

"You spoil these cats rotten."

It's not the observation itself that leaves me so perplexed. Of *course* I spoil my cats rotten. That I do so is an inarguable fact. I spoil them absolutely and unapologetically, and if I have any single regret about it at all, it would only be that I'm not creative enough to come up with even more ways of spoiling them rotten-er. (Suggestions are always welcomed! @ me on Instagram!)

It's the disapproval in my husband's tone that I can't quite grok. I mean, what's even the *point* of adopting a cat—particularly a rescue cat—if it *isn't* to spoil them rotten???

Nevertheless, this self-evident observation is one that's oft repeated in our home. "You're spoiling them," my husband informs me, when I come home from the pet store with an entire shopping bag filled with brand-new catnip toys. "I can't believe how spoiled these cats are," he says ,whenever I prepare little Thanksgiving plate of food for the cats, so they can celebrate along with us. "These are the most ridiculously spoiled cats I've ever seen in my life," he'll insist while watching me cede half my pillow at night to a fuzzy sleeping companion. (Forgetting, perhaps, that the only other cats he's ever spent much time with were the three cats I had when we first moved in together seventeen years ago—three cats who were, I can assure you, just as spoiled then as my current cats are today.)

Sometimes I have to lean in and listen closely to hear his expressions of disapproval, like when I'm in the grocery store carefully evaluating varieties of Temptation treats in order to make sure I only bring home my cats' preferred flavors, while my husband stands next to me shaking his head and muttering, "It is *unbelievable* how spoiled these cats are."

Occasionally I wonder what he thinks is the potential downside of spoiling our cats. Does he worry that I'm not raising them right? That I'm fostering feline narcissism? That when they go out into the world and have to cope with friends and spouses and bosses, they'll be socially maladapted or have unrealistic perceptions of their own importance?

What *exactly* is the harm?

And does my husband honestly think I don't know what's what when I see him coming home with some fancy can of high-end tuna he knows they like, or when he slips Clayton little bits of the turkey from the sandwich he's just made himself, or when—after he thinks I've fallen asleep next to him—he gives Fanny the long and intense late-night back-scratches she craves, while murmuring in her ear, *Who's my pretty girl? Who's a pretty, pretty girl?*

The truth is, there are plenty of people in the world who are selfish or stingy or downright cruel. They're the ones who tend to make the world a worse place to live in. But there are also a handful of us kicking around this big blue marble who take a profound pleasure in making others happy.

And while the business of making other *people* happy (although unquestionably worthwhile!) can be immensely complicated, making a cat happy is usually a much simpler affair—easily accomplished with plentiful chin scritches, a bagful of crunchy treats, and a few strategically placed cushions in sunlit spots around the house.

PAWSOME!

You will never leave your cat

O ver the course of a lifetime, you'll leave homes and schools and jobs and lovers. You'll leave friends you swore you'd never forget and restaurants you used to eat in once a week and at least one teacher who changed your life forever. You'll leave behind yearbooks and schoolbooks and old toys and broken appliances and furniture you spent hours and hours shopping for and shoes that are no longer fashionable and the wildly patterned dishes you bought back when you first got your own place, but that now don't seem quite like "you."

But the one thing you will never—*ever*—leave behind is your cat.

You will never outgrow your cat. You will never try to upgrade your old cat with a newer model. You will never decide that whereas cats used to be all the rage—everybody on TikTok has one!—now they're passé.

You will never ditch your cat because life has gotten too hard or too complicated or too much fun in ways that would make it easier not to have the obligation of caring for a cat. You will never move away and leave your cat behind because moving with a cat is inconvenient, or because you've decided to begin a new life somewhere else, or because maybe you're moving in with someone who doesn't like cats all that much.

How would that even work, anyway? Your cat is your heart, after all. And everybody knows it's impossible to go off somewhere and starat anew while leaving your heart behind.

You'd never even think of trying.

PAWSOME!

You love your cats the way they are

E very cat has their own distinct personality, as any cat lover will tell you. I once lived with a cat who found it intensely unbearable to be in the presence of any human being other than me. At the other end of the spectrum, one of the cats I live with now is so very desperate for human attention that he actually likes going to the vet's office—*where they give him shots*—because at least the person administering the shots is paying attention to him while doing so.

There are cats as happy as the day is long, and cats whose primary personality trait is hostility. There are playful cats and there are prissy cats. There are cats who like to lie in laps, cats who prefer to be lap-adjacent (not so much *on* as *near* their preferred human), and then there are cats who'd rather nap solo. There are cats who love eating "people food," and cats content to stick with their own kibble, thank you very much.

If we're being totally honest, we have to admit that certain qualities are probably objectively better than others. It's better to have a cat who purrs for guests than a cat who's a biter. It's better to have a cat who tolerates the other cats in your house, or who's friendly to the significant other you recently committed to, or who uses the litterbox—and *only* the litterbox—when nature calls.

But, nevertheless...

Ask somebody why they love the person they love, and you're apt to hear things like, "She's smart. She's funny. She's a good friend to her friends." And, sure, those are all legitimate reasons to admire someone.

Here's the great truth when it comes to love, however: While you can always point to the reasons, the reasons aren't the point.

This was a fundamental truth I never fully understood until I came to live with cats and got to know other cat lovers. In twenty-five years, I've never heard a single one say something like, "I love my Buttons because she's so friendly," or "I love Snowflake because he's so playful."

The truth is, we don't love our cats because of specific personality traits they may or may not possess. We love our cats simply because they're ours.

Which is really just another way of saying that cat lovers have been gifted with a tremendous capacity for love—a love that doesn't judge, that doesn't demand, and that doesn't bother trying to look for quasi-logical explanations that don't even matter all that much, anyway.

PAWSOME!

You're your cat's voice and his champion

Wat would your cat do without you?

Who loves your cat like you love him? Who knows your cat like you know him? Who else knows that he's terrified by the sound of a plastic trash bag snapping open? Or that a small, non-descript stuffed worm with a bell in its tail has been his best friend and very favorite toy ever since he was a kitten? Or that, when his tummy's upset, adding a little canned pumpkin to his food is the only thing that makes him feel better?

Nobody—that's who.

Without being too dramatic about it, it's probably fair to say that your love is the only thing standing between your cat and the tender mercies of a frequently cruel world. You're the one who speaks up if a visiting friend's playful children are roughhousing with Buttons a little *too* enthusiastically. And if that too-aggressive play leads your cat to retaliate with a scratch or two, it's you who will speak up in his defense and try to explain what happened from his point of view. *He was trying to tell you he'd had enough when his tail got puffy.*

Scratching and biting are imperfect communications tools, at best—but your cat only uses these tools for lack of any other ability to convey his needs, fears, or desires.

That's where you come in.

The need to act as your cat's interpreter and defender is apt to spring up unexpectedly, in unforeseen ways. You might end up with a significant other who doesn't quite understand or get along with your cat at first. You might have a neighbor who thinks your cat meows too loudly at night and complains to your landlord about it. You might have an exceptionally tidy roommate who doesn't understand *why* there have to be empty paper shopping bags right in the middle of your living room floor.

I've seen three cats through end-of-life illnesses. In each case, their doctor prescribed courses of treatment of varying aggressiveness. Doctors are experts, of course, and their expertise is what we pay them for.

But while a doctor may be an expert on the subject of medical care in general, only *you* are an expert when it comes to your cat. I was ultimately the one who had to consider each recommendation our doctor made in light of the cat that recommendation was for. And I was the one who had to push back when a cat let me know—in ways that were unmistakable, but that nevertheless only I could understand—when that course of treatment was more than the cat in question could handle.

And then I had to do what everybody reading this has had to do for their own cat at some point. I had to find my voice—and I had to use it.

Speaking up to contradict a doctor, or standing up to a significant other, or telling off a roommate or a friend can be difficult. And it's completely understandable if it's the kind of thing you have a hard time finding the courage to do on your own behalf.

When it comes to your cat, though?

You're a gladiator.

You're Braveheart.

You're a downright, honest-to-gosh, take-no-prisoners warrior-hero.

PAWSOME!

You find the strength to let your cat go when it's time

A nd it is—one-hundred percent—the hardest thing you will ever, ever do.

Never doubt for a moment how strong you are for doing it.

PAWSOME

You do thoughtful and completely selfless things for your cat

I 've given it the old college try, but the truth is that no one book could ever truly capture all the manifold and wonderful things you do to make your cat's life just a little bit better on a daily basis.

We've gotten all the way to the end of this book, after all, without even talking about things like how you clean your cat's eyes when they get goopy, or trim their nails (which would otherwise become overgrown and painful) even when they fight you, or pull ticks and burrs—and the occasional wayward price sticker—from their fur, or go to three different stores just to track down that one hard-to-find brand of food they really love.

We couldn't begin to cover in a single book all the times you spontaneously buy your cat a new toy while you're out shopping for other things, or accept with good nature the scratches that your kitty's overly enthusiastic playtimes or cuddle sessions sometimes leave on your hands, or ditch the friends or lovers who say unkind things about your cats that your cats may never hear, but that nonetheless rankle in your own loyal and steadfast heart.

Some of the things you do and the sacrifices you make are huge—like when you forgo that badly needed new pair of shoes so you can pay your cat's medical bills. Some of them are the kinds of small, run-of-the-mill things that are so rarely noticed—like whispering softly in your kitty's ear when she has a bad dream—that nonetheless make up the very substance of a life with someone you love.

But whether they're large or small, difficult or easy, once-in-a-life-time or thoroughly ordinary, never doubt for a moment that even if loving your cat like you do doesn't change the world, it does make the world an infinitely better place for that one little cat.

Actually, scratch that: Making the world better for one little cat is precisely the kind of thing that—were everyone to do it the way you do—*would* make the whole world better for all of us.

But you already knew that.

PAWSOME!

Read the instant *Times* bestseller published in 22 languages!

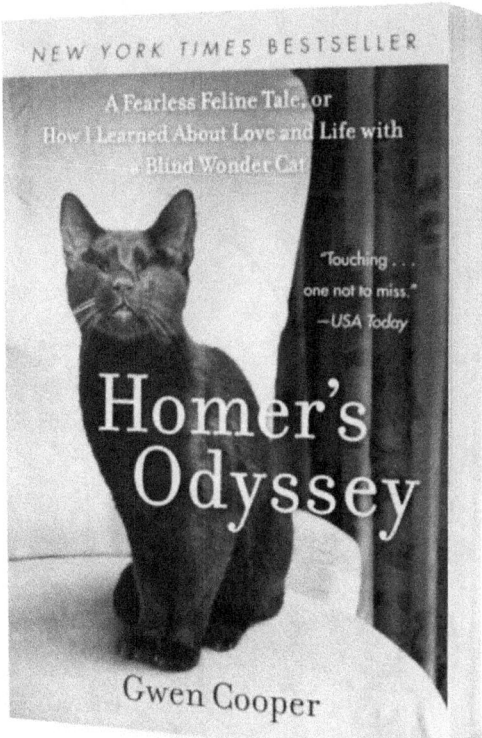

"This is one of the most heartwarming, touching and inspirational stories you'll ever read! A love story like no other between a truly amazing, utterly fearless little blind cat and his adoring Mom!"
-Amazon Reviewer

———— ⊹ ⊹⊹ ⊹ ————

Heartfelt thanks and profound gratitude to the following people (and cats!), without whom I could never have completed this book.

Special thanks to Patti, Nikolaka & Koa!

- » Alyson Amsterdam (and Louie & Biggie)
- » Margaret Auld-Louie (and Julius & Simba)
- » Jamery Sue Barry (and Colby, Sully, Misty & Georgie)
- » Charles Brackney (and Shane, Chloe & Abby)
- » Julie Burns
- » Lisa Calarese (and Riley, Mordecai & Rigby)
- » Nicole Ciffolillo-Grubbs (and Ralphy)
- » Deborah Foresman (and Tinkerbell)
- » Paul Froiland (and Louie & Fitzy)
- » Meg Galipault (and Scout, Waffles, Sisu, Dru & Huckleberry)
- » Lee-Ann Gilliam
- » Tracy Ginnane
- » Wanda Goodwin (and Lewie Stewart)
- » Jill Graves
- » Susan Haenicke (and Bessie & Hamilton)
- » Marianne Harding (and Charles Carlos Ambrose Harding)
- » J. Eric Hoehn
- » Susan Anne Kadlec
- » Julie Kennedy

- » Connie Keith-Kerns (and Zoey, Ari Kai & Mrf)
- » Calvin & Eileen Keyser (and Ashes, Ninja & Snickers)
- » Beth Kirby
- » Ken Kistner
- » Ronald Koltnow (and Speedy)
- » Catherine Larklund
- » Louisa Lee
- » Carole Loftin (and Sadie, Biscuit & Brazil)
- » Julie Lowe (and Gracie, Cougar, Java, Raven, Meeko, & Bella)
- » Neta Mercer (and Pouncer, Felix & Snacks)
- » TJ Murphy (and Shelly, Max, Gio & Anna)
- » David Nagreski (and Chassis)
- » Matthew O'Leary (and Hank)
- » Melanie Paradise (and Idia)
- » Stephanie Peters (and Max)
- » D.H. Powell IV (and Bobby & Willow)
- » Vanessa Ramirez
- » Stephanie Reicen (and Oliver, Mickey & Helen)
- » Kathryn Rigsby
- » Felicia Roe (and Eurydice & Cassiopeia)
- » Janice Rogenski
- » Kathy Schlichthernlein (and Scrappy & the Gang)
- » Zoe Shinno (and Midnite)
- » Christine Sorenson
- » Emily Stafford (and Randy & Pepper)
- » Anne Teghtmeyer
- » Lenai Waite (and Martin)
- » Allison Walls (and Podo, Rue & Dom)
- » Katie Williams
- » Michele Zarichny

Gwen Cooper is the *New York Times* bestselling author of the memoirs *Homer's Odyssey: A Fearless Feline Tale, or How I Learned About Love and Life with a Blind Wonder Cat*; *Homer: The Ninth Life of a Blind Wonder Cat*; and *My Life in a Cat House: True Tales of Love, Laughter, and Living with Five Felines*, as well as the novel *Love Saves the Day*, narrated from a rescue cat's point of view. Her work has been published in more than two-dozen languages. She is a frequent speaker at shelter fundraisers and donates 10% of her royalties from *Homer's Odyssey* to organizations that serve abused, abandoned, and disabled animals.

Gwen lives in New Jersey with her husband, Laurence. She also lives with her two perfect cats—Clayton "the Tripod" and his litter-mate, Fanny—who aren't impressed with any of it.

**To learn more about Gwen and her books,
visit www.gwencooper.com**